THE GUIDE TO
HOLLYWOOD
AND BEVERLY HILLS

THE GUIDE TO *Hollywood* AND BEVERLY HILLS

The Best Driving Tours, Walks, Restaurants, Homes, Shopping, Sights, and Architecture

CHARLES LOCKWOOD

CROWN PUBLISHERS, INC.

Grateful acknowledgment is hereby made to
Warner Bros. Inc. for use of lyrics from
"Boulevard of Broken Dreams" by Al Dubin and Harry Warren
© 1933 (renewed) Warner Bros. Inc.
All rights reserved.
Used by permission.

Credits for photographs in inserts following pages 14, 46, 110, and 142.

FIRST INSERT
First page: All courtesy of the Bruce Torrence Historical Collection. *Second page:* Both courtesy of the Marc Wanamaker/Bison Archive. *Third page:* All by David A. Gardner. *Fourth page: Top and left:* David A. Gardner. *Bottom cameo:* Courtesy of the Los Angeles Public Library. *Bottom:* Courtesy of The Frank Lloyd Wright Memorial Foundation.

SECOND INSERT
First page: Both by David A. Gardner. *Second page:* All by David A. Gardner. *Third page:* Both by David A. Gardner. *Fourth page:* All by David A. Gardner.

THIRD INSERT
First page: Both by David A. Gardner. *Second page:* David A. Gardner. *Third page:* Both by David A. Gardner. *Fourth page: Top:* Courtesy of Marc Wanamaker/Bison Archive. *Bottom:* Courtesy of the California Historical Society/Tico Insurance Co. (Los Angeles).

FOURTH INSERT
First page: Top: Randolph Harrison. *Bottom:* Author's collection. *Second page:* All by David A. Gardner. *Third page: Top:* Randolph Harrison. *Bottom:* David A. Gardner. *Fourth page: Top:* Courtesy of The Huntington Library. *Bottom:* Randolph Harrison.

Published by Crown Publishers, Inc.,
One Park Avenue, New York, New York 10016, and
simultaneously in Canada by General Publishing Company Limited
Manufactured in the United States of America
Library of Congress Cataloging in Publication Data
Lockwood, Charles.
The guide to Hollywood and Beverly Hills.
Includes index.
1. Hollywood (Los Angeles, Calif.)—Description—Guide-books.
2. Los Angeles (Calif.)—Description—Guide-books.
3. Beverly Hills (Calif.)—Description—Guide-books.
I. Title.
F869.H74L62 1984   917.94'94   83-14341
ISBN 0-517-55036-9
Book design by Camilla Filancia
10 9 8 7 6 5 4 3 2 1
First Edition

Contents

Acknowledgments

Although it is the author's name that always appears on the title page, all books are collaborative efforts, and this one is no exception. The following people generously showed me their favorite parts of Hollywood and Beverly Hills, gave me information and photographs, or provided moral support: Douglas Bartoli, Max Butler, Crosby and Linda Doe, Gary Freeman, Paul and Pam Garnett, Marion Gibbons, Randy Harrison, Ian Hollister, John Isern, Richard Lamparski, and Marc Wanamaker.

I was triply fortunate to have worked with Maxine Groffsky, my literary agent in New York; Barbara Grossman, the book's editor at Crown; and David Groff, her assistant. The book reflects many of Barbara's wise suggestions.

David A. Gardner deserves special mention. He took most of the book's contemporary photographs, and these sensitively depict present-day Hollywood and often reveal the most familiar sights from a fresh perspective. Thank you, David.

I dedicate this book to Lawrence R. Barker, whose friendship has always meant so much to me since we met as freshmen at Princeton University nearly twenty years ago.

Introduction:

How to Use This Book

This is a personal guide to Hollywood, Beverly Hills, and Bel Air: their architecture, flora, history, restaurants, shops, and topography. But this book is not an exhaustive description of every last building, place to eat, or view. Instead it focuses on what I believe to be the places and things that are really special as well as those that typify Los Angeles, whatever their quality or fascination.

In making these selections and writing my observations, I cannot claim to be a lifelong Angeleno. I have lived here since 1979. But I do have the perspective of someone who has chosen to settle in Los Angeles—despite its smog and dependence on the automobile—after having lived in Washington, D.C., New York, and San Francisco. Being a five-year resident, I know Hollywood well enough to share some of my favorite sights, yet I still remember the excitement and occasional bewilderment that first- or second-time visitors often feel.

Introduction

This guidebook has eleven chapters. The first is a brief history of Hollywood. The second describes its climate and topography. Then come nine chapters about specific parts of town: starting with Hollywood Boulevard, followed by the Hollywood flats, lower Hollywood Hills, upper Hollywood Hills, Sunset Strip, West Hollywood, Melrose Avenue, Beverly Hills, and Holmby Hills/Bel Air. Each of these nine chapters begins with a brief description of what the area is like, then it locates and describes the various sights. Unlike some guidebook writers who give everything equal coverage, I have decided that the more interesting the place, the longer the commentary.

How can you find the information you want in this guide most easily? Let's say that you are a movie buff who has longed to see Hollywood Boulevard for years. Just locate Hollywood Boulevard in the general index at the end of the book and turn to those pages. You'll find plenty of architectural, historical, movie, restaurant, and shopping information. If visiting Rodeo Drive, the Sunset Strip, or Bel Air is your heart's desire, look up those geographic areas in the index as well.

What if your interests are more specific, such as the architecture buff who came to Hollywood to look at buildings? Or maybe you are a bicoastal businessperson who wants to take an Angeleno associate out for a good lunch in Beverly Hills. Perhaps you are a couple on vacation seeking a rustic spot for hiking.

At the beginning of each entry in this book, you will find a symbol in bold type which classifies that sight's primary appeal. The little building 🏠 stands for architecture. An old-fashioned movie camera 🎥 stands for the motion picture industry. A crossed knife and fork ✕ is a restaurant. A palm tree 🌴 is flora, topography, or open space. A small rectangle with a $ in the middle $ is a shop. The masks of comedy and tragedy 🎭 stand for entertainment. And an open book with a capital *H* in the middle 📖 is history.

Introduction

Some sights are important for more than one reason. The Chinese Theater on Hollywood Boulevard, for instance, has a movie camera and a building symbol, because it is an architectural landmark as well as a motion picture buff's shrine.

Thanks to these symbols, you can quickly locate points of personal interest without reading each entry. Let's say that you are the architecture devotee who plans to be in the Hollywood flats. To locate the entries for the nearest architectural attractions, just look for the little building symbols in that chapter. If you're the hungry bicoastal businessperson who will be on Rodeo Drive, turn to the Rodeo Drive pages and find the crossed knives and forks.

Now that you know how to find all this information, what's the best way to explore Hollywood, Beverly Hills, and Bel Air? You can take the city buses, but this is time-consuming and the Southern California Rapid Transit District (commonly called RTD) doesn't service many of the rustic areas like the Hollywood Hills or Bel Air. To get the most out of your visit, you simply need a car, whether you drive your own into town or rent one from an agency.

Once you have a car, buy a detailed street map at a newsstand or bookstore, in order to supplement those in this book. Better yet, if you are an AAA member, stop at an Automobile Club of Southern California, show your membership card, and get their excellent "Central and Western Area" map, which includes Hollywood, Beverly Hills, and Bel Air, among other districts.

If you use this guide and plan your sightseeing carefully, you need not spend all your time in Hollywood behind a steering wheel. For some areas in this guide, like Hollywood Boulevard or Rodeo Drive, you will find a point-by-point walking tour (plus recommended places to park your car), which includes a selection of restaurants where you can eat lunch or simply have a snack and rest your feet. Other sections of town, like Melrose Avenue, West Hollywood, or the Hollywood flats, are not arranged as walking tours because the sights are scattered over a long street or large geographic area. By studying the guide, however, you can discover a cluster of attractions that interest you, drive over to that vicinity, and see everything on foot before returning to your car and heading to the next destination.

Introduction

For some hillside districts like the Hollywood Hills, Benedict Canyon in Beverly Hills, or Bel Air, this guidebook offers point-by-point driving tours, which include detailed directions so that you don't have to refer to the map constantly. These hillside driving tours mention many places where you get out of the car and enjoy a particularly fine view, take a walk in a rustic setting, or have a picnic.

Contrary to what some out-of-towners think, Hollywood is not all that difficult to find your way around in. Just think of Hollywood and neighboring West Hollywood as a grid that is subdivided by major east-to-west streets, namely Franklin Avenue, Hollywood Boulevard, Sunset Boulevard, Santa Monica Boulevard, and Melrose Avenue, and important north-to-south thoroughfares like Vermont Avenue, Western Avenue, Vine Street, Highland Avenue, La Brea Avenue, Fairfax Avenue, Crescent Heights Boulevard, La Cienega Boulevard, and Robertson Boulevard. On pages 2–3, you will find a map which highlights these streets.

How do you use these major thoroughfares to go from one place to another? Assume you are exploring some of the residential streets just south of the Beverly Hills Hotel and want to eat lunch at the City Café on Melrose Avenue several miles away. First, find the restaurant's address in this guidebook. It's 7407½ Melrose. Then see where this number falls on the Melrose Avenue map. City Café is located between Fairfax and La Brea avenues.

But how do you get there? Study the overall Hollywood, Beverly Hills, and Bel Air map on pages 2–3 and plot the most direct route to the City Café, using the major thoroughfares. This may not always be the fastest route, but it is the easiest for the visitor to follow. If you want to reach the City Café from the area just south of the Beverly Hills Hotel, for instance, drive south to Santa Monica Boulevard, turn left and proceed eastward on Santa Monica Boulevard until you reach Doheny Drive and make the gentle right onto Melrose Avenue. Then head eastward on Melrose, past Robertson, past La Cienega, past Crescent Heights. Only when you cross Fairfax Avenue, do you have to look for building numbers in order to locate the City Café.

Introduction

While driving around Los Angeles, you will quickly realize that the highway department wants to make life easy for the motorist. At most intersections on busy thoroughfares, separate turn lanes allow you to wait for the opposing lane of traffic to pass without holding up the entire lane of traffic to the rear. On major avenues, moreover, easily read large blue signs announce the upcoming street from half a block away.

Remember two driving rules that may be different from those in your hometown. First, pedestrians have the right of way. Once someone steps into a crosswalk, you must stop, even if the street is full of traffic and no stoplight is near. Second, you may turn right on a red light *if* you have come to a complete stop, *if* you are in the right-hand lane, *if* no traffic is coming in the lane you want to turn onto, AND *if* no sign prohibits the turn on red. You can also make a left-hand turn from a one-way street onto another one-way street.

Now that you have learned how to get around Los Angeles, you deserve to know the best news of all: It doesn't take a lot of money to enjoy Hollywood. Sure, it helps to be rich—or at least a well-paid professional—if you want to eat at fancy restaurants or buy a lot of clothes. And this guide does recommend the best places to do this. But you can go to chic restaurants and shops in most large cities. The things that make Hollywood such a special place to visit don't cost much, such as enjoying the magic of the movie industry's golden era, driving by incredibly landscaped million-dollar celebrities' homes, or exploring an undeveloped canyon just minutes from Hollywood Boulevard. And who can put a price on Hollywood's marvelous climate? Instead of lots of money, what you really need in Hollywood is curiosity, open-mindedness, and stamina in order to discover the places and things that make this community almost unique among large American cities.

THE GUIDE TO
HOLLYWOOD
AND BEVERLY HILLS

1
A History of Hollywood

Originally the home of the Cahuenga Indians, later part of the Rancho La Brea land grant, the section of Los Angeles which is now known as Hollywood had become several farms and ranches by the nineteenth century. But rapid changes took place during the Los Angeles real estate boom of the late 1880s.

In 1887 Horace Henderson Wilcox decided to turn his ranch into a new town, and he mapped his barley fields and orange groves into streets, blocks, and lots. As a show of faith, Wilcox built his own gabled and turreted mansion on the dirt road that he grandly named Wilcox Avenue. It was Wilcox's wife, Daeida, who called the town Hollywood after the country estate of a friend back East, or so the story goes.

Horace and Daeida Wilcox hoped that Hollywood would become more than just a real estate venture. As devout Methodists and active Prohibitionists, they had an almost Utopian vision of a Hollywood that would become a model of Christian virtue for the still violent, vice-ridden Los Angeles. The Wilcoxes barred sa-

1

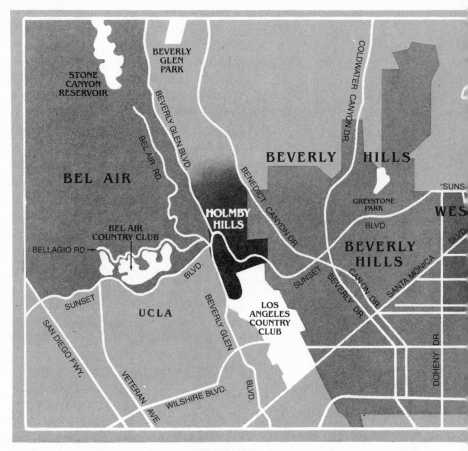

loons and liquor stores and offered a free lot to any church willing to locate in Hollywood. Unfortunately, only a handful of
houses had been built in Hollywood when the Southern California land boom collapsed in 1889. Horace Wilcox died the following year. Daeida Wilcox married Philo Judson Beveridge in 1894
and continued to donate free land to religious and community
organizations, but Hollywood became a backwater with about
600 residents, whose main excitement was waiting for the stage
from Los Angeles or watching tourists at C. J. Sketchley's Ostrich
Farm or the Cahuenga Water Gardens, where Edward D. Sturte-
vant raised water lilies that were large enough for a child to
stand upon.

Shortly after the turn of the century, Hollywood started growing again, because an electric trolley now provided regular ser-

2

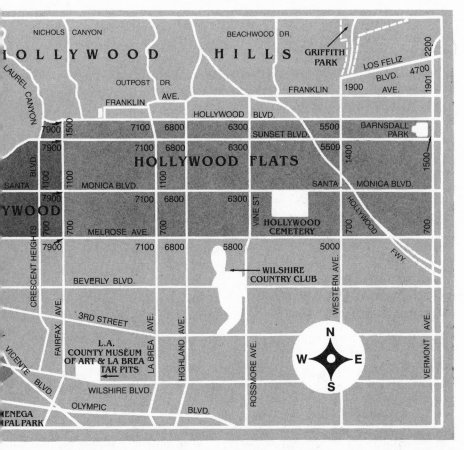

vice to Los Angeles, seven miles to the southeast. As more and more Los Angelenos and retired Middle Western farmers built homes in Hollywood, the community incorporated as a city in 1903. That same year, the original part Moorish/part Spanish thirty-three-room Hollywood Hotel opened on unpaved Hollywood Boulevard between Orchid and Highland avenues. By 1910, Hollywood's population had reached 4,000 souls, most of whom were the sober, church-going middle-class folk of whom Horace Wilcox would have approved.

But quite a surprise awaited Hollywood's residents. In 1911, the Centaur company, owned by David and William Horsley, rented the empty Blondeau Tavern at the corner of Sunset Boulevard and Gower Street to make silent movies. Within the next few years, half a dozen other production companies worked spo-

3

radically in Hollywood, just as several dozen more had come to Los Angeles from the East Coast and Middle Western studios to take advantage of the nearly year-round warm, sunny weather and the varied scenery within a day's journey.

Most Hollywood residents did not like this influx of movie companies one bit. They called the studios "gypsy camps," and boardinghouse keepers posted signs saying "NO DOGS AND NO ACTORS." In 1910, the Hollywood city fathers banned all movie theaters in the town.

The reasons for this antagonism were many. The movie companies came from places like New York City, and that alone was enough to worry the retired Middle Western farmers who moved out to Hollywood because Los Angeles was the wicked big city. Most actors and actresses, furthermore, had worked on the stage before getting into the movies, and all "theater people" were morally suspect, according to prevailing middle-class mores.

Old-fashioned bigotry also played its part. Hollywood's residents generally were white Anglo-Saxon Protestants whose families had been in this country for generations. But most movie company leaders—men such as William Fox, Samuel Goldwyn, Carl Laemmle, and William Selig—were Jewish or foreign-born, and sometimes both.

The movie companies, of course, brought some of this trouble on themselves. Early production companies worked so quickly turning out ten-minute one-reelers and twenty-minute two-reelers that they didn't have time to build elaborate sets in the studio: It was quicker and cheaper to use all of Hollywood as a big movie set. Many families' quiet Sunday outings were ruined when movie companies borrowed Griffith Park for country settings. Filming chase sequences invariably tied up traffic on Hollywood Boulevard. Sometimes movie companies paid a family five dollars to film a scene at their front door, but more often a housewife heard strange noises and found an entire production company working on the front lawn.

The worst offenders were the film companies making Westerns. The movies may have been silent, but the noise of gunfire, cowboy whoops, and horses' thundering hooves during the filming were not. Many cowboy extras were real-life cowboys who didn't see any distinction between what they did for the camera and what they did after work. At the end of the day, they sometimes raced their horses down Hollywood's quiet suburban streets, screaming and taking potshots at the palm trees.

Indignant Hollywood families couldn't do much about the movie companies, because their town had traded its municipal sovereignty for a steady supply of water and become a part of Los Angeles in 1910. And growth-obsessed Los Angeles business and civic leaders were not going to restrict any industry, no matter what they personally may have thought about the production companies' behavior or the movie people's morals. A group called the Conscientious Citizens, for instance, collected more than 10,000 signatures on petitions asking the city council to run the movie companies out of Los Angeles, to no avail.

By 1920, public attitudes about the movie companies had changed considerably, and not just because of the nationwide moral and social loosening after World War I. Moviemaking was becoming an important industry throughout Hollywood and all Los Angeles, employing thousands of extras, set carpenters, and wardrobe mistresses. Thousands more young men and women had come to Hollywood in hopes of working in the movies or even becoming actors and actresses.

From the 1920s onward, many Hollywood residents idolized the movie stars, who were America's leading media heroes in the days before widespread radio and television programming. And some of the more devoted fans "staked out" certain Hollywood homes, studios, restaurants, and nightclubs in hopes of glimpsing, perhaps even talking to, their favorite celluloid idols.

Today, the motion picture industry has largely deserted Hollywood proper for other parts of Los Angeles and the nation. More than ever before, Hollywood is another part of the sprawling Los Angeles metropolitan region. Office buildings, shops, and cheap to middle-class housing fill the flats. Costly homes dot the Hollywood Hills. But Hollywood has not forgotten its glorious cinematic past. Turn a corner, and you may see Charlie Chaplin's studio, the "footprints of the stars" in front of the Chinese Theater, or the HOLLYWOOD sign. For millions of Americans, and millions more people around the world, Hollywood will always be synonymous with the movies.

2
Climate and Topography

Few American cities enjoy a finer natural setting than Los Angeles or the Hollywood district, seven miles northwest of the downtown area. Los Angeles is located on a flat coastal plain next to the Pacific Ocean, whose nearly constant offshore breezes ensure a mild and predictable climate. In summer and early fall, the thermometer rarely rises above eighty-five degrees, and even after the warmest days, it usually drops into the sixties for the evening. In winter, the daytime temperature typically reaches the sixties and often higher, but at night it usually falls no lower than forty degrees. Freezing weather and snow are virtually unknown.

Los Angeles receives an average of fifteen inches of rain a year, and almost all this precipitation comes from winter storms off the ocean. Sunny mornings frequently follow an evening rainfall, and on these days the air is washed to a brilliant clearness and the grass and chaparral-covered hills are green and glisten with moisture. When the rainy season ends in March or April, the hillsides turn golden brown and become dry, and canyon residents anxiously worry about the danger of fire until the rains return late that fall.

The city's most famous topographical feature is the Santa Monica Mountains, which begin near downtown Los Angeles and stretch 15 miles westward to the Pacific Ocean, thereby dividing the coastal plain from the inland San Fernando Valley. Reaching 3,059 feet at their highest point, these mountains are still the home of rabbits, skunks, deer, rodents, rattlesnakes, dozens of species of birds, and brazen coyotes which rummage through hillside dwellers' garbage and sometimes carry off their pet cats and small dogs.

In the Hollywood district, the Santa Monica Mountains are known as the Hollywood Hills, where expensive 1920s Spanish haciendas, mock-Tudor mansions, and modern homes look down—literally as well as figuratively—on the business streets, the cheaper bungalows, and the apartment buildings in the "flats" below. Hidden away in the Hollywood Hills are rustic canyons, with names like Laurel, Nichols, and Beachwood, where residents feel as if they are living in the country even though Hollywood Boulevard is a ten-minute drive away.

In clear, smogless weather, the view from the Hollywood Hills or along almost any stretch of the Santa Monica Mountains is breathtaking: To the south lies the coastal plain, bathed in sunlight and filled with the city's buildings and freeways. To the east, the view focuses on the growing cluster of downtown office towers, and to the southwest is the sparkling, sailboat-flecked Pacific Ocean and Santa Catalina Island, located 27 miles offshore, with mountains rising over 2,000 feet above the sea.

Behind the Santa Monica Mountains lies the 22-mile-long San Fernando Valley, the second flat plain inland from the Pacific Ocean and now an endless series of suburbs with names like Studio City, Sherman Oaks, Encino, and Woodland Hills. Because the Pacific Ocean breezes usually don't get past the Santa Monica Mountains, "the Valley" often is ten degrees hotter than the coastal plain in summer and about five to ten degrees cooler in winter. But the Santa Susana and San Gabriel Mountains, which form the Valley's other long boundary and constitute the second mountain chain from the ocean, do protect the San Fernano Valley and the coastal plain from much of the desert heat and dust in the even hotter and drier Central Valley, which is the third inland plain.

For several days every September and October, however, the cooling ocean breezes die down, and the gusty Santa Ana winds come out of the desert, filling the air with grit and bringing Los Angeles its hottest and driest days all year. The already-parched hillside chaparral turns into potential tinder, and Los Angeles' worst brush fires break out.

Although nature blessed Los Angeles with this remarkable climate and topography, it was man who turned the landscape green. The secret ingredient was water. Originally, the coastal plain was dusty grassland and the Santa Monica Mountains were barren except for patches of chaparral on the steep hillsides and clumps of small trees near occasional streams in the canyons. But around 1870, Los Angelenos discovered artesian water beneath the coastal plain, and in subsequent decades they brought water to their city from the Owens Valley and the Colorado River.

By the late nineteenth century Los Angelenos turned their coastal plain and the San Fernando Valley into a veritable Garden of Eden. The palm tree, eucalyptus, acacia, pepper, and fragrant night-blooming jasmine, which seem to have always been a picturesque part of the local landscape, were actually imported to Los Angeles. Thousands of farmers planted vegetable patches, barley fields, orchards, and citrus groves. In March and April, tens of thousands of orange, grapefruit, and lemon trees bloomed, and when the night mist off the ocean held this scent close to the ground, the air smelled like perfume.

Air quality no longer is one of Los Angeles' enviable features. Thanks to the otherwise-beneficial mountains and sunshine, industrial pollution and automobile exhaust are trapped, then cooked, in the coastal plain and, therefore, Los Angeles suffers the worst air pollution of any major American city, especially during the late summer and early fall months.

But smog's curse does not weigh equally on all parts of the

city. Near the coast, in Santa Monica and Venice for instance, the air is reasonably clean, because the offshore breezes push the pollution inland. That prevailing wind pattern means bad air in Hollywood, which is ten miles from the coast, but the pollution is even worse farther inland or in the virtually land-locked San Fernando Valley.

Because of their sheer numbers and frequent thoughtlessness, people have spoiled the near-perfect physical setting that they helped create in Los Angeles one hundred years ago. But even the unhealthy yellowish-brown smog, the soaring population, and too many cars cannot totally obscure Los Angeles' extraordinary climate and topography. And if you explore the winding streets of the Hollywood Hills on warm summer evenings, you can still find those near-magical places where the air is truly sweet, thanks to the profusion of night-blooming jasmine and pittosporum planted along the roads and around the houses.

3 Hollywood Boulevard

BACKGROUND

During the 1920s and 1930s, no part of Los Angeles was more glamorous than the one-mile stretch of Hollywood Boulevard between La Brea Avenue and Vine Street, which was lined with movie theaters, restaurants, nightclubs, stylish shops, and hotels. All across America, millions of movie fans longed to stroll up and down the Boulevard, in hopes of seeing their favorite actor or actress walk out of a restaurant and get into a waiting car, and they dreamed of standing outside one of the movie palaces at a première and watching the stars step out of their limousines, as photographers' flashbulbs exploded one after another and searchlights crisscrossed the darkened skies.

Alas, this Hollywood Boulevard no longer exists. With almost no exceptions, the fine restaurants and shops have closed or moved farther west to West Hollywood and Beverly Hills. The hotels and apartment buildings on the Boulevard and along the nearby side streets have become badly run down. And movie stars or television personalities are never to be seen, except perhaps in a passing car. A handful of movie theaters are about the only things that remain much the way they once looked.

Today Hollywood Boulevard is frequently called the Times Square of Los Angeles, because it has more than its share of fast-food joints, greasy spoon coffeeshops, flashy but cheap clothing stores, X-rated movie theaters, tourist-trap souvenir shops, and empty storefronts. On weekdays, the sidewalks and the street are oddly quiet for a major thoroughfare. But on warm weekend evenings, thousands of young people from East Los Angeles and the San Fernando Valley crowd the sidewalks or cruise up and down the street in their cars, seeing and being seen.

Nevertheless, Hollywood Boulevard is *not* doomed to a continuing downward spiral. In addition to its world-famous name and the splendid sights which attract millions of tourists every year, it is one of the few places where Los Angelenos can get out of their cars and walk around without feeling that they are out of place. Hollywood Boulevard is wide enough to be grand looking, but not so wide that the roadway visually and functionally separates one side of the street from the other. The line of 1920s and 1930s buildings on both sides of Hollywood Boulevard clearly defines the street's space, and with few exceptions they are not so tall that they block the sun from the amply wide sidewalks. And above the modern storefronts, many Hollywood Boulevard buildings are splendid Spanish- or Art Deco-style architectural gems.

Perhaps more important for any eventual revival, Hollywood Boulevard is well located in present-day Los Angeles, an easy drive from the burgeoning downtown financial district and the San Fernando Valley. Nearby West Hollywood and the even-closer winding residential streets of the Hollywood Hills contain some of the most desirable real estate in Los Angeles. And if once-lowly Melrose Avenue and part of the Silverlake district can experience a renaissance, why can't Hollywood Boulevard?

11

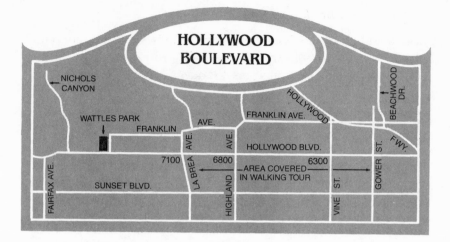

HOLLYWOOD BOULEVARD

NICHOLS CANYON

WATTLES PARK

FRANKLIN AVE.

FRANKLIN AVE.

HOLLYWOOD

BEACHWOOD DR.

FRANKLIN AVE.

HOLLYWOOD BLVD.

FWY.

7100   6800   6300
—AREA COVERED—
IN WALKING TOUR

FAIRFAX AVE.   SUNSET BLVD.   LA BREA AVE.   HIGHLAND   VINE ST.   GOWER ST.

Park in one of the lots just above or below Hollywood Boulevard on Orange or Sycamore streets. Begin the walking tour at the Chinese Theater, 6925 Hollywood Boulevard.

MANN'S CHINESE THEATER   *6925 Hollywood Boulevard.*
Telephone: 464-8111.

Of all the Hollywood Boulevard theaters, unquestionably the most famous is Mann's Chinese, the one with the footprints of the stars in cement out front. When the Chinese Theater opened in 1927 with the première of Cecil B. DeMille's *King of Kings,* then-owner Sid Grauman proclaimed that the building was "authentic in every detail," and so it must have seemed with the Oriental curio shops arranged around the sides of the forecourt and the 30-foot-high dragon above the pagodalike entrance. Inside the nearly all-red lobby and auditorium, more dragons and Chinese motifs decorated the carpets, chairs, walls, and even the ceiling. On either side of the movie screen stood bronze and crystal pagodas. To complete the Oriental theme, the bathroom faucets resembled dragons.

Although the gilt paint is peeling off the columns in a couple of places, the Chinese Theater still is a great place to see first-run movies. And with its large screen, six-track Dolby stereo system, and opulent architectural setting, the Chinese makes the

12

stripped-down new theaters in the Beverly Center or in West-wood seem about as charming as a high school auditorium.

FOOTPRINTS OF THE STARS   *At the forecourt of Mann's Chinese Theater, 6925 Hollywood Boulevard.*

If any single place symbolizes the enduring magic of the Hollywood legend, it is the forecourt of the Chinese Theater. All day long, crowds come here to see the stars' footprints in cement, a tradition which began when Douglas Fairbanks, Sr., and Mary Pickford accidentally stepped on a just-poured sidewalk in front of the theater and Sid Grauman, always the showman, asked them to sign their names.

In the passing years, more than 160 stars have left their footprints in cement at the Chinese Theater. But for some actors and actresses, footprints were not enough. John Barrymore's square includes his famous profile. Betty Grable pressed one of her legs into the wet cement. Roy Rogers' square has Trigger's horseshoe print. A few stars even wrote short greetings; Joan Crawford scratched, "To Sid, may this cement our friendship."

Although most of the stars' footprints date from the 1920s, 1930s, and 1940s, the forecourt of the Chinese Theater offers something for just about everyone. Old men and women slowly wander from square to square, quietly lost in their memories of equally aged or now-dead stars. Other people try the stars' footprints for size. "I didn't realize that her feet were so tiny" is one often-heard comment. And some visitors dash around the forecourt looking for their favorites. "Mommy! Mommy!" shrieks a thirteen-year-old girl. "Here's John Travolta! And Sylvester Stallone!"

The tourists come and go, but one man never leaves his post near the theater entrance. Like the guardian of an ancient temple, he monotonously calls out several words again and again, half muffled by the background noise of passing buses and cars on Hollywood Boulevard. What's he saying? Move closer, and you'll hear the words "Movie star home tours! Movie star home tours! Tickets here!"

13

WALK OF FAME *On Hollywood Boulevard from Gower to Sycamore streets and on Vine Street from Sunset Boulevard to Yucca Street.*

In the late 1950s, the Hollywood Improvement Association tried to bring some glamour back to already-fading Hollywood by installing over 2,500 brass-trimmed pink terrazzo stars in a new gray terrazzo sidewalk along one mile of Hollywood Boulevard and several blocks of Vine Street. According to the promoters' plan, each star would include a different celebrity's name in brass, plus a miniature brass movie camera, radio microphone, record, or television set to signify how the stars achieved their stardom.

In 1958, the first eight stars were dedicated at the northwest corner of Hollywood Boulevard and Highland Avenue, and they honored Olive Borden, Ronald Colman, Louise Fazenda, Preston Foster, Burt Lancaster, Edward Sedgwick, Ernest Torrence, and Joanne Woodward. How many of these names can *you* recognize?

Today, the Walk of Fame stars honor over, 1,700 entertainment figures. But rather than lending much excitement to Hollywood Boulevard, as the well-meaning promoters intended, the Walk of Fame is a gum-stained reminder of what the street once was.

VISITORS' INFORMATION *6801 Hollywood Boulevard, northwest corner of Highland Avenue. Open Monday–Thursday, 9:00 A.M. to 4:00 P.M., and Friday, 9:00 A.M. to 6:00 P.M. Closed Saturday and Sunday.*

MUSSO & FRANK GRILL *6667 Hollywood Boulevard, just east of Highland Avenue, a few blocks west of Cahuenga Boulevard. Monday–Saturday, 11:00 A.M. to 11:00 P.M. Telephone: 467-7788. Moderate. All major credit cards. Parking in rear.*

TOP LEFT: *Horace Wilcox, 1887;* TOP RIGHT: *Daeida Wilcox, 1887.* BOTTOM: *The first map of Hollywood, prepared by Horace and Daeida Wilcox as they started selling building lots in the fledgling community in 1887.*

TOP: *A scene from* The Squaw Man *(1913), one of the movie industry's first nationwide box office successes. Notice the Hollywood Hills in the background of this outdoor set.* BOTTOM: *By the 1920s, movie studios were scattered throughout the Hollywood "flats," often looking like small factory buildings. These "extras" are awaiting their call about 1920.*

TOP LEFT: *Hollywood Boulevard revels in its past glories. This is a memorabilia shop window next to the Pantages Theater.* TOP RIGHT: *Hollywood Boulevard today: the Frolic Room near the restored Pantages Theater.* BOTTOM: *"Footprints of the Stars" in front of Mann's Chinese Theater, 6925 Hollywood Boulevard.*

TOP: *Being the land of "make believe," Hollywood appropriately has the suitably picturesque cemetery. This Greek temple is millionaire William A. Clark, Jr.'s tomb at the Hollywood Memorial Park Cemetery. Actress Marion Davies is buried in the smaller white marble mausoleum beneath the trees to the right.* LEFT: *Frederick's of Hollywood's naughty pink and purple Art Deco palace, 6608 Hollywood Boulevard.* BOTTOM CAMEO: *Aline Barnsdall, the eccentric oil heiress, who hired Frank Lloyd Wright to design her Hollyhock House atop a knoll rising above the Hollywood "flats."* BOTTOM: *The living room at Aline Barnsdall's Hollyhock House about 1920. Frank Lloyd Wright designed both the house and much of its furniture.*

Open since 1919, the Musso & Frank Grill bills itself as the oldest restaurant in Hollywood, and during the 1930s and 1940s it was a hangout for writers like William Faulkner, F. Scott Fitzgerald, and Ernest Hemingway, who had come to Hollywood to write for the movie studios.

Today Musso's is nothing less than a citywide institution, and it is packed nightly with young men and women trying to make it in show business, people who have made it in show business and talk nothing but, middle-aged couples headed for the theater, even old-timers who remember when. For people who are eating alone, Musso's even has a comfortable counter where you can watch the cooks at work.

At one time, Musso & Frank's was one of Hollywood's finest restaurants, but its part American/part Continental meals have slipped, just like the surrounding stretch of Hollywood Boulevard. Even so, you'll never go really wrong with anything on the vast menu, which is printed daily, and often the food can be quite good and filling. To be on the safe side, try one of the simpler dishes such as steak, lamb chops, Sauerbraten with potato pancakes, one of the broiled fish selections, or an omelette. The flannel cakes are justly famous for breakfast, if you don't mind eating breakfast after the restaurant opens at 11 A.M. And where else can you find a large dining room which has hardly changed since its 1937 redecoration or gruff, quick-moving waiters who seem to have worked there almost that long?.

$ ■ BOOKSELLERS' ROW ■ *North side of Hollywood Boulevard from Highland Avenue to Cahuenga Boulevard.*

If you are looking for a book that was published more than a year ago, you probably won't find it in one of the chain bookstores, which try to turn over their "product" several times a year. But don't give up hope. You probably can find the book—and save some money—at one of the stores that sell used books along the north side of Hollywood Boulevard between Highland Avenue and Cahuenga Boulevard.

For most subjects, your best bet is Book City, 6627 Hollywood Boulevard, a large, well-organized store whose books are clean and often virtually new. For movie titles, photographs, and memorabilia, also check Bennett's Books, 6753 Hollywood Boulevard, whose Italian Renaissance palazzo-style 1922 building was the site of the celebrity-filled Montmartre Café in the 1920s and 1930s.

U.T.B. BUILDING   *6605 Hollywood Boulevard.*

Why can't commercial buildings look this good today? This three-story 1926 structure reflects the Spanish Colonial Revival style in all its glory: red tile roof, arched windows deeply set into stucco walls, wrought-iron balconies, even some elaborate Churrigueresque ornament, which is named for a family of Spanish architects who added further embellishments to the already-elaborate Spanish Baroque style.

IVAR STREET SIDE TRIP

If you are curious and energetic—remember that you still have the other side of Hollywood Boulevard to see—turn left on North Ivar Street. The block above Hollywood Boulevard isn't much to look at. But the second block, which starts climbing uphill just past Yucca Street, is a well-preserved period piece of 1920s and 1930s architecture, including a bungalow court of small frame cottages, in the half-timbered mock-Tudor style, the Moderne style, and the Spanish style.

This block of North Ivar has been the home of several well-known Hollywood celebrities, in fact and in fiction. During 1935 Nathanael West lived in the Parva-Sed Apartments at 1817, while he wrote scripts for B movies, and it was here that he got the idea for writing *The Day of the Locust*. While staying at the Parva-Sed, West became friends with many of the prostitutes who lived in the building. West frequently drove the women back and forth to their clients. Returning the favor, the prostitutes sewed buttons back on his shirts and helped him wash his dishes.

Farther up the hill, Marie Dressler lived in the large Spanish-style house at 1850, where North Ivar Street ends at a steep, ivy-covered hill above Franklin Avenue. Marie Dressler was a silent screen star whose career ended in the late teens, but Lazarus-like she returned to the movies a decade later and became an even bigger star in such MGM comedies and dramas as *Anna Christie, Tugboat Annie,* and *Dinner at Eight.*

Across the street at 1850 North Ivar, fans of the 1950 film *Sunset Boulevard* will recognize the Spanish-style Alto Nido Apartments as the home of struggling young screenwriter Joe Gillis, played by William Holden, before he stumbles into the eerie fantasy world of Norma Desmond, a once-renowned but now-almost-forgotten half-mad silent movie star, played by Gloria Swanson. If *Sunset Boulevard* was being made today, this lovely three-story red-tile-roofed building would not need any "architectural makeup" to look like the place where an unsuccessful screenwriter would live. The stucco walls are faded. The shutters have fallen off the windows, and the windowframes badly need paint.

"HOLLYWOOD AND VINE"

Can this shabby-looking intersection really be the famed Hollywood and Vine? Look what occupies the four corners: a one-story Howard Johnson, the former Broadway department store, the Hollywood–Vine Drugstore, and the Hollywood Equitable Building. Nothing is happening at Hollywood and Vine today, and nothing much happened here forty or fifty years ago. But the mystique which still clings to Hollywood and Vine does prove one thing—the infinite power of good publicity. But isn't that what Hollywood has always been about?

CAPITOL RECORDS BUILDING   *1750 Vine Street.*

If you think that Los Angeles' fling with "symbolic architecture"—that is, hot dog stands that resembled a hot dog in a bun—ended in the 1930s, take a look at the thirteen-story Capitol Records Building, which was completed in 1956 on Vine Street just above Hollywood Boulevard. What could be more appropriate for a record company than a circular building that looks like a gigantic stack of records? And don't miss the chimney on top that looks like a stylus.

CHAO PRAYA   *6307 Yucca Street, just west of Vine Street. Sunday—Thursday, noon to midnight; Friday—Saturday, noon to 1:30 A.M. Telephone: 464-9652. Inexpensive. All major credit cards.*

Going to Chao Praya for the first time takes some courage. This Thai restaurant, which also serves Chinese and some other Southeast Asian dishes, is located on a desolate stretch of Yucca Street, surrounded by empty storefronts and parking lots, a block north of Hollywood Boulevard. The slightly shabby dining room won't win any design prizes either.

But it's the good, often imaginative food and the low prices, not the ambience, that makes this restaurant such a welcome find in this part of Hollywood. Taking its inspiration from various Oriental cuisines, Chao Praya offers soups, fried noodle dishes, rice dishes, meat and seafood entrées, plus Thai specialties like *pa nang* (beef, coconut milk, curry, and chili), *pa rarm* (pork with vegetable topped by satay sauce), or *larb* (ground beef and hot chili with vegetables).

Be sure to try Chao Praya's popular barbecued chicken, and don't forget to read the day's several blackboard specials which typically might be chicken with green beans, curry roast duck, frogs' legs with garlic sauce, and crab meat with asparagus. By the time you have eaten all this delectable and sometimes fiery food, and have paid your preinflation-level check, you'll know why so many Hollywood residents return to Chao Praya again and again, even if it sometimes means waiting on line out the front door on weekend evenings.

PANTAGES THEATER   *6233 Hollywood Boulevard. Telephone: 469-7161.*

Whatever else you see along Hollywood Boulevard, don't miss the Pantages Theater, located just east of Vine Street. Built as a movie palace in 1930 and converted into a legitimate theater for stage plays and musicians six years ago, the Pantages was the first Art Deco-style movie house in America, and remarkably it still retains every exuberant bit of its architectural details, both inside and out.

The part masonry, pary black marble façade has typically Art Deco zigzag grillwork, stylized sunbursts and plant motifs, and Egyptian statues peering down from the rooftop parapets. Inside, the lobby is an 18-foot-high rounded vault, supported by richly ornamented and spot-lit columns. At either end of the lobby are broad staircases with a matched set of statues on each side which portray a woman pilot wearing goggles and a scarf and a movie director standing behind his camerman. Be sure to look up at the very Deco sunbursts above the elevator doors. The vast 2,288-seat auditorium, which was the location for the Academy Awards from 1949 to 1959, is an almost-unbelievable jumble of columns and typically rectangular sharp-edged Art Deco ornament, which are overlaid with vaguely neoclassical and Byzantine motifs.

Rather than just admiring the Pantages' architecture, go to a show here, and you will understand something of what people experienced in the 1920s and 1930s when they saw a film in one of Hollywood's movie palaces: strolling through the palatial lobbies, being taken to their seats by uniformed ushers in the even more fantastically decorated auditoriums, and finally being spellbound by the larger-than-life images of the stars on the silver screen and becoming lost in reveries of what it would be like to be that good-looking, that rich, and that popular.

SITE OF THE CECIL B. DEMILLE BARN STUDIO *Southeast corner of Selma and Vine streets. See entry on page 47.*

BROWN DERBY *1628 North Vine Street, one block south of Hollywood Boulevard. Lunch, Monday–Saturday, 11:00 A.M. to 2:00 P.M.; dinner, Tuesday–Saturday, 5:00 P.M. to 11:00 P.M.; Sunday brunch, noon to 3:00 P.M. Valet parking. Telephone: 469-5151. Moderate. All major credit cards.*

Thirty or forty years ago, the Vine Steet Brown Derby was one of the hottest spots in Hollywood, particularly when the nearby studios let out for lunch. Movie stars and radio personalities held court at their tables, and Hollywood columnists like Hedda Hopper and Louella Parsons scurried around the dining room, collecting tidbits of gossip which would titillate their faithful readers the next morning.

Although Hedda and Louella are gone, along with some of the highly charged atmosphere, the Brown Derby is otherwise surprisingly unchanged. The spacious dining room has the same red banquettes, large crystal chandeliers, and seeming hundreds of caricatures covering the walls as it did in its heyday. You may still see some real-live stars. And the kitchen serves the same extensive American-style menu. All the meals are good, though not great; the best bet is the justly famous Cobb salad (named after former maître d' Bob Cobb), which contains lettuce, watercress, celery, tomato, avocado, chicken, bacon, and Roquefort cheese, all finely chopped together.

TERRIFIC TRIO *6608, 6602, 6562–6554 Hollywood Boulevard.*

Perhaps Hollywood Boulevard's precipitous decline hasn't been entirely for the worse after all. If the street had remained fashionable after World War II, these three remarkable buildings probably would have been remodeled or torn down, in order to keep up with changing architectural tastes or rising property values. But here they stand today, in much their original 1920s and 1930s glory.

The several stores at 6562–6554 Hollywood Boulevard embody the Spanish Colonial Revival style, with a few Moorish arches thrown in for good measure. The two-story J. J. Newberry Building at 6602 is a 1928 Art Deco masterpiece of turquoise tile with beige-and-butterscotch-color tile trim. Walk inside. The interior is almost unchanged.

Next door, at 6608, you can hardly miss Frederick's of Hollywood's three-story white- and pink-trimmed, purple-painted Art Deco store, which was built for S. H. Kress & Co. in 1935. Decades ago, Frederick's naughty negligees and revealing dresses provided untold fantasies for young women across America. But that was before *Playboy* and the sexual revolution. With its smart, landmark-quality building, Frederick's is almost respectable these days.

EGYPTIAN THEATER   *6708 Hollywood Boulevard. Telephone: 467-6167.*

In Hollywood Boulevard's heyday during the 1920s and 1930s, probably the most exotic-looking theater was Sid Grauman's Egyptian, which reportedly was modeled after the Temple at Thebes and opened in 1922 at the height of the public excitement over the discovery of King Tut's tomb. The theater stood about 100 feet back from Hollywood Boulevard, and to reach the heavily columned entrance, moviegoers walked down a long dramatically decorated courtyard which had imitation stone walls in stucco, mock tombstones, and larger-than-life paintings of Egyptian deities.

The lobby boasted more fake stone blocks, paintings of Egyptian scenes, and vaguely Egyptian furniture, plus brightly painted statues of pharaohs and mummy cases which looked as if they came from a studio's prop department. Inside the vast auditorium, heavily decorated columns and sphinxes stood guard on either side of the stage, and an enormous metallic vulture sat atop the screen. The sunburst grillwork which extended from its outstretched wings concealed the organ grill.

The Egyptian Theater, unfortunately, has changed for the worse since the 1920s when the usherettes dressed like Cleopatra and a costumed guard paraded back and forth atop the parapet overlooking Hollywood Boulevard. Although the theater is still a good place to see movies, it has a neglected and unloved look, and thanks to several misguided renovations in recent decades, it is neither Egyptian nor up-to-date and modern. Ernesto's Italian Restaurant and Pizzeria somewhat incongruously occupies one corner of the still vaguely Egyptian forecourt, and inside the lobby a lone video game stands next to a forlorn-looking mummy case.

YANGZEE DOODLE CHINESE CAFE *6776 Hollywood Boulevard. Monday–Saturday, 11:30 A.M. to 9:30 P.M. Telephone: 464-0071. Inexpensive.*

This is just the kind of restaurant that Hollywood Boulevard—and hungry visitors—need: a fast-food establishment that is clean, cheerful, good, and inexpensive. Yangzee Doodle's storefront is glass brick, and the dining room has a high-tech look, done predominantly in black and white. All day long, the restaurant serves a dozen hot dishes, some of your usual Chinese fare, some not. For Chinese fast food, all the meals are tasty and, will wonders never cease, the meals are served on stoneware, not plastic or paper plates.

 MAX FACTOR MAKE-UP SALON *1666 North Highland Avenue.*

Few buildings look more "Hollywood" than the Max Factor Make-Up Salon, which was designed by S. Charles Lee in the early 1930s. The building essentially follows the Art Deco style with its characteristic symmetry for each part, the flat roof and parapets, and the vertical bands as ornament. But Lee, a some-time theater architect, fancied up the building with stylized ancient Greek flower motifs, neoclassical swags, even all-American stars.

"THE BOULEVARD OF BROKEN DREAMS"

Jack Warner decided to remove the following sequence from Warner Brothers' 1933 film *Footlight Parade* because it was "too depressing."

HE: When on the sidewalk I see—
SHE: Pardon me, but aren't you Dick Powell?
HE: Yes, I'm Dick Powell.
SHE: I wonder if you'd, do me . . . I thought maybe *(sob)*—
HE: Here, here, here— What's the matter?
SHE: Oh you wouldn't understand. Hollywood's been good to you!
HE: What do you mean?
SHE: Oh, I guess it's an old story. . . . There was a beauty contest in Little Rock. I won it. Came to Hollywood to win fame. Instead—I'm on Hollywood Boulevard at two in the morning. And no place to go. *(sob)*
HE: Oh, poor kid. Why don't you go home? I'd be glad to help—
SHE: Oh I can't go home a failure. You wouldn't understand but—
HE: But what?
SHE: Well, it may sound silly after all the disappointments I've had, but I know that all I need is a break. If I could get just one real chance—
HE: Well, isn't there anyone at home who misses you?
SHE: There . . . There's a boy there. He works in a garage, and he's a swell guy. He—he—wants to marry me.
HE: Well listen, kid, you've got more than anything *Hollywood* can offer you. You know, there are lots of girls you envy . . .

who only wish a swell guy was waiting for *them* in Little
Rock. Or anyplace else for that matter.

SHE: I guess you're right, Mr. Powell. Huh—and I thought Hollywood was a boulevard of beautiful dazzling dreams—

HE: But I'm afraid you're *dead* wrong!

(Then Dick Powell sings:)

I walk along the street of sorrow
The Boulevard of Broken Dreams
Where Gigolo—and Gigolette
Can take a kiss—without regret
So they forget their broken dreams
You laugh tonight and cry tomorrow
When you behold your shattered schemes
And Gigolo—and Gigolette
Wake up and find their eyes are wet
With tears that tell of broken dreams—

Here is where you'll always find me
Always walking up and down
But I left my soul behind me
In an old cathedral town.
The joy that you find here you borrow
You cannot keep it long it seems.
But Gigolo—and Gigolette
Still sing a song
And dream along
The Boulevard of Broken Dreams

4
Hollywood Flats

BACKGROUND

Roughly bounded by Franklin Avenue on the north, Vermont Avenue on the east, Melrose Avenue on the south, and Fairfax Avenue on the west, the "Hollywood flats" is not one of the prettiest or best-kept sections of Los Angeles, but it is one of the most varied and vital, both physically and socially.

The major east-to-west streets like Santa Monica or Sunset boulevards and the north-to-south thoroughfares like Western or Highland avenues are a jumbled mixture of television and movie studios, shops, parking lots, gas stations, office buildings, and restaurants, from all different vintages. Turn off one of these traffic-filled boulevards onto one of the narrower side streets, however, and the cityscape changes dramatically. Some streets combine 1920s bungalows, prewar Spanish-style duplexes and quadruplexes, and rambling three-story postwar

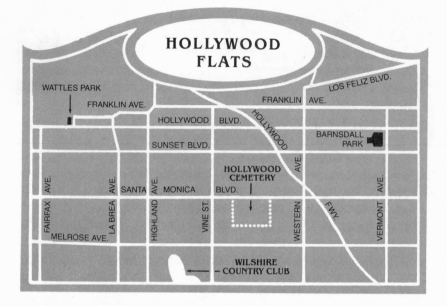

HOLLYWOOD FLATS

apartment buildings, all ranging in condition from near perfect to downright shabby. Other blocks are solidly lined with frame or stucco bungalows, which sit back from the street behind well-trimmed lawns and look as if they came from a Middle Western town.

This seeming case of architectural mistaken identity isn't all that surprising, because many of Hollywood's 1920s and 1930s residents were Middle Western farmers and small businessmen, who had retired in Southern California's pleasant climate. In more recent years, the Hollywood flats has attracted different kinds of newcomers. Some are young men and women, hoping for a break in show business. But most are now Latin, Middle Eastern, or Asian immigrants who are looking for a more basic kind of opportunity.

In the midst of Hollywood's bustling commercial activity and its vibrant, sometimes-disconcerting ethnic caldron, sharp-eyed visitors will find some familiar Los Angeles landmarks like Crossroads of the World or the Frank Lloyd Wright-designed Hollyhock House. You will also see well-loved motion picture industry relics like the old Paramount gates or the Charlie Chaplin studios, which often stand next to the modern studios that give the Hollywood flats so much of its vitality today.

HOLLYWOOD MEMORIAL PARK CEMETERY   *6000 Santa Monica Boulevard, just east of Gower Street.*

Isn't this where the heavily veiled "Lady in Black" used to bring flowers to Rudolph Valentino's tomb every year on the anniversary of his death? True enough. The silver screen's greatest lover, who starred in *The Sheik, Blood and Sand,* and *Son of the Sheik,* is buried in crypt 1205 in the Court of the Apostles.

Valentino has plenty of company from Hollywood's golden age. This cemetery is the final resting place of Marion Davies (whose white marble mausoleum is marked Douras, her original last name), Cecil B. DeMille, Nelson Eddy, Jesse Lasky, who produced *The Squaw Man* (which was the first major film made in Hollywood), Peter Lorre, Adolphe Menjou, Constance Talmadge, and Norma Talmadge, plus more recent figures like Peter Finch, Tyrone Power, and Carl "Alfalfa" Switzer.

Probably the grandest tomb is Douglas Fairbanks, Sr.'s neoclassical white marble mausoleum, which sits in a sunken garden at the end of a long rectangular reflecting pool filled with water lilies. Mary Pickford reportedly paid for Fairbanks, Sr.'s impressive tomb, even though she and "Douglas" had been divorced for nearly four years at the time of his death in 1939. Mary's ashes are buried near her mother, brother, and sister at Forest Lawn Cemetery in Glendale.

But Hollywood Memorial Park is more than just the cemetery of the old-time stars, plus thousands of ordinary and not-so-ordinary Los Angelenos. It is one of the few open spaces in this densely built up part of the Hollywood flats. Too bad the cemetery doesn't permit picnics. The green lawns, all kinds of trees and flowering shrubs, and the lake—complete with a Greek templelike tomb on a small island—make this a relaxing place to visit, particularly after driving around Los Angeles.

You can get a free map at the Administration Building just inside the Santa Monica Boulevard gate.

VISTA THEATER *4473 Sunset Drive. Telephone: 660-6639.*

Revival theaters were few and far between in Los Angeles ten years ago and most classic film buffs faced the unhappy choice of seeing their favorites constantly interrupted by commercials on television or not seeing them at all. This is no longer true. In the last few years, Los Angeles has experienced a revival-theater boom, not just in Hollywood, but in Long Beach, Pasadena, and the San Fernando Valley as well. Some of these theaters started showing classic films out of love for old Hollywood. Others switched to revivals, because they were failing as second- or third-run houses.

One of the most popular revival theaters is the Vista. The Vista was built as a neighborhood movie and vaudeville house in 1923, started showing Russian-language films in the 1950s, and switched to gay sex films in the 1970s, before screening classics in 1980. Check out the theater lobby and interior. What could be more fun than seeing old movies in a theater that still has its original King-Tut's-tomb-has-just-been-discovered Egyptian interior?

For other Los Angeles revival theaters, see the Calendar Section supplement of the *Sunday Los Angeles Times* or read *Los Angeles Weekly.*

SITE OF D. W. GRIFFITH'S SETS FOR *INTOLERANCE* (1916)
4500 Sunset Boulevard.

When Los Angeles builders embarked on their architectural free-for-all following the First World War, they had to look no further than the local movie theaters for ideas: Chinese. Mayan. Egyptian. Eighteenth-century French. No style—or combination of styles—was too farfetched. But the movie studios also provided inspiration for Los Angeles' architectural eclecticism with their outdoor sets. The wood-and-plaster Coliseum for the first *Ben Hur* (1925) and the Middle Eastern domes and minarets of

Douglas Fairbanks, Sr.'s *The Thief of Baghdad* (1924) loomed over Los Angeles' squat bungalows and dusty suburban streets years after the films were completed.

But the grandest outdoor set ever built in Hollywood was the massive Babylon for D. W. Griffith's flawed masterpiece, *Intolerance,* which depicted man's inhumanity to man in four different historical eras. The 100-foot-high towers and temples for Griffith's celluloid Babylon remained standing for years, thereby providing inspiration for architects and builders all over Los Angeles, until the Fire Department ordered the studio to demolish the crumbling lath-and-plaster structures.

[$] **CROSSROADS OF THE WORLD**   *6671 Sunset Boulevard,*
[🏠] *extending through the block to Selma Avenue.*

Thanks to Southern California's easy climate, the presence of flamboyant theaters and outdoor movie sets, and the absence of a strong local architectural tradition, Los Angeles architects and builders embarked on an orgy of eclecticism in the 1920s and 1930s that was unmatched in any other American city: Pseudo-Egyptian bungalow villages; part Spanish, part Venetian, part Gothic shops; half-timbered Tudor mansions shaded by distinctly un-Tudor palm trees.

One of the most whimsical and most successful examples of this eclectic frenzy is Crossroads of the World, a collection of shops and offices completed in 1936. From the main entrance along Sunset Boulevard, the central building looks like an elegant streamlined ocean liner, except that its roof sprouts a very 1930s-looking tower, topped by a revolving ball, which symbolizes the world. The rest of Crossroads of the World is a European village, which consists of English, French, and Spanish cottages standing next to one another.

[🏠] **HOLLYWOOD HIGH SCHOOL**   *2051 Highland Avenue,*
[🎥] *northwest corner of Sunset Boulevard.*

Hollywood High may look like many other aging big-city

schools. But you know this isn't so, because Hollywood has never been just another big-city neighborhood. In keeping with its location, Hollywood High has graduated dozens of movie and television stars, beginning with Fay Wray, class of 1924, who is best remembered for playing the blond damsel-in-distress in *King Kong* (1933). Other celebrated show business alumni include Jason Robards '39, Nanette Fabray '40, Carol Burnett '51, Sally Kellerman '55, Linda Evans '60, Stefanie Powers '60, and John Ritter '66.

Hollywood High's most famous student, Lana Turner, née Judy Turner, never graduated at all. She attended the school for only a month and a half. One afternoon in January 1936, Lana cut her tenth-grade typing class and went to the nearby Tip Top Café, which used to stand at the northeast corner of Highland Avenue and Sunset Boulevard.

While the already-alluring auburn-haired Lana was drinking a Coke, Billy Wilkerson, the publisher of the *Hollywood Reporter*, asked her if she wanted to become an actress in the movies. "I don't know," Lana replied. "I'll have to ask my mother." Apparently, Mother said Yes, because Lana signed a contract with MGM and played supporting roles in *They Won't Forget* (1937) and *Love Finds Andy Hardy* (1939) before she emerged as one of Hollywood's most popular stars in the 1940s.

If Lana Turner returned to Hollywood High today, she would hardly recognize the place except for some of the attractive 1930s Moderne-style buildings. The student body, which was once overwhelmingly white, is mostly black, Mexican, and Asian. Hookers patrol nearby Sunset Boulevard—in broad daylight, no less. Yet Hollywood High's current appearance may be deceiving. Who knows when one of the more recent graduates will become a star?

KCET STUDIOS *4400 Sunset Drive. One-hour guided tours are available on Tuesdays and Thursdays by appointment only. Telephone: 667-9242.*

The public television station KCET occupies one of Los Angeles' oldest studios, which started out as a small lot where the Lubin Company filmed silent Westerns in 1912. And the KCET Studios are one of the least-changed production facilities in Hollywood, as you can see from some of the 1920s red-brick buildings along the street. But this studio never was one of the vast "dream factories" like Paramount or MGM. Instead, it usually was a hardworking rental lot, and its most famous films were Monogram Pictures' Charlie Chan, East Side Kids, and Bowery Boys series of the 1940s and 1950s.

Finding KCET can be difficult. Sunset Drive, which is the studio's address, is not Sunset Boulevard. At Virgil Street, which is several blocks east of Vermont Avenue, Sunset Boulevard turns right at an angle in order to head downtown. If you continue straight ahead, east of Virgil, the street is Sunset Drive, and the KCET Studios are located on your right shortly thereafter.

PINK'S CHILI DOGS   *709 North La Brea Avenue, just north of Melrose Avenue. Open seven days, 8:00 A.M. to 2:00 A.M. Telephone: 931-4223. Inexpensive.*

Although you won't find Pink's in any Los Angeles restaurant guide, this is a serious chili hot dog stand. Just look at the quickly moving line that forms during meal hours. Besides hot dogs, the menu includes hamburgers, tamales, pie, coffee, and soda. You can take your food to one of the small tables inside or on the patio. Or you can eat your chili dog at a stand-up counter, like many Pink's regulars.

CHARLIE CHAPLIN STUDIOS/NOW A&M RECORDS
1416 North La Brea Avenue.

When Charlie Chaplin became a star in the late teens, he built his own studio on La Brea Avenue, which then was a mixture of vacant lots, houses, and shops. But not just any kind of architecture would satisfy the multimillionaire "Little Tramp." To recall his British origins, Chaplin designed his studio to look like a picturesque row of half-timbered cottages. Starting with *A Dog's Life* (1918), Chaplin made all his films here, including classics like *The Kid* (1920), *The Gold Rush* (1925), *City Lights* (1931), *Modern Times* (1936), and *The Great Dictator* (1940). From the moment that Chaplin moved into this studio, it became a mecca for his fans. So many men and women waited outside the main entrance all day long for a glimpse of their hero that Chaplin often entered and left by the side door on De Longpre Avenue, just off La Brea.

Herb Alpert and Jerry Moss's A&M Records purchased and restored the Chaplin Studios in 1966. Bravo.

FRANK LLOYD WRIGHT IN HOLLYWOOD *Aline Barnsdall's Mayan-inspired HOLLYHOCK HOUSE (1919–1921), 4800 Hollywood Boulevard, just east of Vermont Avenue. Open to the public. Admission charge. Tours every Tuesday and Thursday, 10:00 A.M. to 1:00 P.M. every hour on the hour, and the first Saturday and Sunday of each month, noon to 3:00 P.M. every hour. For information, call 662-7272.*

What was Frank Lloyd Wright doing in Hollywood during the late teens and why did he design a sprawling Mayan-inspired mansion? Hadn't Wright already won international acclaim shortly after the turn of the century for the strongly horizontal earth-toned Prairie Houses that he built in the Chicago area and throughout the Middle West?

Yes, Wright had, but he also wanted to make major changes in his career after the First World War. Quite correctly, Wright had felt that he was typecast as the Prairie House architect, because his practice depended on a narrow base: the substantial free-standing house for the upper-middle-class family living in a comfortable Middle Western town. By the late teens, however, American life and architectural tastes were undergoing major changes. Increasingly, Wright saw the careers of his architectural contemporaries begin to fade: architects like Purcell and

Elmslie in Chicago, or Irving Gill, Greene and Greene, and Bernard Maybeck in California, who clung, despite the tenor of the times, to the dying Arts and Crafts tradition and usually designed suburban houses.

The Prairie Houses represented these outdated values, and Wright knew that his career would suffer unless he caught up with the new society and the architectural tastes that were emerging in the wake of the First World War. Wright was fifty years old in 1917, but that did not daunt him from beginning a long struggle to broaden his architectural vision.

By the late teens, Wright also wanted to improve his painful personal life. In 1909 he had left his wife and family to live with Mamah Borthwick Cheney, the wife of a former client, at his home in Spring Green, Wisconsin, which he named Taliesin. But when Wright was working in Chicago on August 15, 1914, his momentarily deranged butler set fire to Taliesin, thereby destroying the house and killing seven people, including his beloved Mamah.

For both these professional and personal reasons, Wright welcomed Aline Barnsdall's invitation to design her new Hollywood home, even though he knew that she was a headstrong and opinionated oil heiress, who had left her husband in Chicago in 1916 and had moved to Los Angeles, where she managed the Little Theater on South Figueroa Street.

Los Angeles didn't know what to do with the thirty-five-year-old Barnsdall. She smoked in public. She wasn't divorced from her husband but insisted on using her maiden name. And after she bought the 36-acre Olive Hill, which rose 100 feet from the coastal plain in eastern Hollywood, Aline Barnsdall announced plans to build her home on top and to establish an artists' colony and cultural center on the lower slopes, thereby rescuing Los Angeles from its cultural deprivation.

In contrast to his earlier Middle Western work, Frank Lloyd Wright let his eclectic architectural fantasies run free in Los Angeles, and he designed Aline Barnsdall's 6,200-square-foot residence as a Mayan temple, built of poured concrete and stucco over wood framing and decorated with the hollyhock motif that she so dearly loved. He also planned a theater, rehearsal studios, and a lecture hall with a rooftop restaurant near the lake along the Vermont Avenue side of the hill. He laid out artists' studios and actors' residences on the hillsides below Hollyhock House.

After several years of wrangling with Wright over architectural matters, Aline Barnsdall moved into the completed Hollyhock House in September 1921 with her daughter, several servants, and twelve dogs. But before Wright could finish more than two nearby guesthouses, Aline Barnsdall called a halt to the hillside cultural center, and in December 1923 she offered Hollyhock House and the top 10 acres of Olive Hill to the City of Los Angeles. Although she publicly cited tax considerations for her decision, Aline Barnsdall probably felt that her new home's countrified charms were slipping away as the orange groves and barley fields below Olive Hill quickly gave way to bungalow subdivisions, which were certainly no vista for a confirmed aesthete.

After initially refusing Aline Barnsdall's offer, the City of Los Angeles accepted the 10-acre property in 1926, and the California Art Club leased Hollyhock House. But the city did not set aside adequate maintenance money, and when the California Art Club moved out of Hollyhock House in 1941, the building was literally disintegrating, thanks to water-rotted beams and geological shifts in Olive Hill.

Hollyhock House sat empty until Dorothy Murray, a Los Angeles woman who had been active in the USO and whose son had been killed in the Second World War, turned the building into a recreation facility for service men and women in 1946. Although Mrs. Murray was not interested in architecture and actually disposed of the original Wright-designed furniture, she did rescue Hollyhock House from impending destruction. Ten years later, in 1956, the city belatedly realized Hollyhock House's national importance, took back the lease from the R & R facility, and started a restoration, which continues to this day, in fits and starts.

Although Hollyhock House lacks most of its original furniture and the eastern slope of Olive Hill is a shopping center named Barnsdall Square, this is still one Hollywood landmark that should not be missed. According to the American Institute of

Architects, Hollyhock House is one of seventeen Frank Lloyd Wright buildings that must be preserved at all costs as an example of his contribution to American architecture.

When visitors reach the entrance on Hollywood Boulevard, the hilltop mansion is still hidden from view, just as nonconformist and intensely private Aline Barnsdall had intended. The driveway winds up the hill several times along the way, past several hundred trees, into a courtyard on the north side of the house. Once visitors reach this point, Hollyhock House still maintains its privacy, because the building is oriented in the three other directions, and a narrow, low-ceilinged 40-foot covered walk leads to the forbidding front doors, which are made of concrete and weigh 250 pounds each.

But just past these massive doors, guests enter a low-ceilinged welcoming entrance hall with the dining room located on the left and up two steps. Wright designed the hexagonal dining table, which sits in the room today, because he believed that six was the right number of people for dinner. The six matching oak chairs have backs of rectilinear panels which create a sort of trellis for a spine of stylized hollyhock carvings to stand against.

The bright and spacious living room, though lacking its Wright-designed furniture, is the most impressive room in the house. French doors along the west wall open onto a terrace overlooking the city and the Pacific Ocean. The double-height ceiling has white, tan, and lavender panels, which suggest the sand, mountains, and sunsets of the Southwestern desert. The fireplace is an abstract sculpture, in relief, of favorite Wright motifs, such as overlapping disks and squares with a brief nod at the vertical hollyhock forms. A half-hexagonal apron juts out from the hearth over a pool of water that reflects flames from the fire. When the hearth was cold, this pool mirrored patterned daylight from an intricately latticed skylight overhead.

Don't stop here. See the rest of the house and its secluded courtyard, then wander around the grounds, and if you have time, visit the nearby Municipal Art Gallery. See the entry on the Barnsdall Municipal Art Gallery, which follows.

NOTE: For Frank Lloyd Wright's next Hollywood building, see the John Storer residence on page 38.

BARNSDALL MUNICIPAL ART GALLERY *4804 Hollywood Boulevard. Admission charge. Open Tuesday–Saturday, 12:30 P.M. to 5:00 P.M. Tours at 2:00 P.M. Telephone: 660-2200.*

Situated near Hollyhock House, this gray concrete gallery, which was designed by Arthur Stevens in 1971, displays the work of Los Angeles artists in every medium. Around Christmastime, exhibits are prepared for children. The gallery's theater hosts films and concerts.

5

Lower Hollywood Hills Tour

BACKGROUND

Thanks to its elevated yet convenient location just above the "flats," the lower reaches of the Hollywood Hills between Laurel Canyon and Los Feliz Boulevard started to develop as a fashionable residential district in the teens and 1920s. Since then, the Hollywood Hills have remained a desirable place to live, but they have never become so chic that most of the houses have been drastically enlarged or modernized, as has happened in much of Beverly Hills.

Consequently, the lower Hollywood Hills are an architectural and historical treasure trove with houses ranging from occasional turn-of-the-century frame cabins to literally hundreds of 1920s and 1930s Spanish-style mansions, plus some works by nationally revered architects like Frank Lloyd Wright, Richard Neutra, and Rudolph Schindler. The natural sights include steep and majestically barren hillsides, a still-undeveloped canyon,

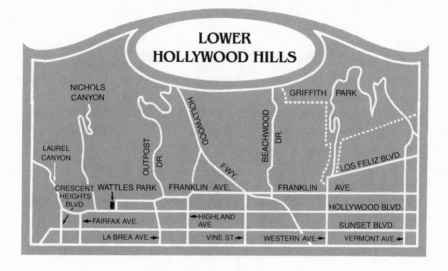

LOWER
HOLLYWOOD HILLS

NICHOLS
CANYON

GRIFFITH PARK

HOLLYWOOD

BEACHWOOD
DR.

LAUREL
CANYON

OUTPOST
DR.

LOS FELIZ BLVD.

FWY.

CRESCENT WATTLES PARK   FRANKLIN AVE.   FRANKLIN   AVE.
HEIGHTS
BLVD   HOLLYWOOD BLVD.

←FAIRFAX AVE.   ←HIGHLAND
                       AVE.   SUNSET BLVD.

LA BREA AVE.→   VINE ST.→   WESTERN AVE.→   VERMONT AVE.→

and some of the best parks in Los Angeles, not to mention stunning views from the hills of the city below.

NOTE: The following tour requires two hours of driving on narrow and winding hillside roads.

LOWER HOLLYWOOD HILLS   *START: Laurel Canyon Boulevard and Hollywood Boulevard.* NOTE: *Crescent Heights Boulevard becomes Laurel Canyon Boulevard near Hollywood Boulevard.*

MILEAGE: *15*

TIME: *Three hours*

As you drive north on Crescent Heights/Laurel Canyon Boulevard, get over into the left-hand lane. One block beyond the stoplight at Hollywood Boulevard, drive into the left-turn lane, and carefully make a U-turn so that you are heading south again. Immediately get into the right-hand lane, then make a slight right turn onto Hollywood Boulevard. Why do you have to follow all these complicated directions? Because you cannot legally make a left turn onto Hollywood Boulevard from Crescent Heights/Laurel Canyon Boulevard.

Several hundred yards ahead on your right, you will see the *JOHN STORER RESIDENCE,* 8161 Hollywood Boulevard, which

38

was designed by Frank Lloyd Wright. Private residence.

After completing Aline Barnsdall's Mayan-inspired Hollyhock House in 1921, Frank Lloyd Wright invented a new construction technology, the so-called textile-block, as another way to adapt his architectural repertoire to the post-First World War world. In all, Wright completed four textile-block houses in the Los Angeles area during the early 1920s. The first was Mrs. George Madison Millard's "La Miniatura" in Pasadena, and the following three textile-block houses were built in Hollywood, beginning with the rather grand John Storer residence.

Although these four houses differ in many ways, they all share certain construction and design elements. Not only the exterior but also the interior walls were made of precast hollow concrete blocks, some of which were plain-surfaced, others perforated or covered with deeply textured abstract geometric designs. The concrete blocks were joined with steel tie-rods, which meant that walls made from them could accommodate great compression and tension forces and were earthquake-resistant. Moreover, the walls were durable, excellent insulators, and easy to build.

The John Storer residence consists of a living room, dining room, and four bedrooms, and it is situated on a residential stretch of Hollywood Boulevard which runs along the base of the Hollywood Hills. Even though this city lot did not offer much seclusion, Wright managed to fit the house into the hillside, and it became a man-made extension of the landscape with its varied silhouette, numerous terraces, and extensive landscaping.

Because of its large size, the Storer residence also gave Wright considerable flexibility in design. The rooms and terraces, for instance, were at different levels, thereby permitting both a free, visually exciting massing of the façade and a spatial fluidity inside. The house's focus, moreover, was a large two-story living room, opening onto two roof-garden terraces which overlooked the city.

After viewing the Storer residence, make a U-turn on Hollywood Boulevard, cross Crescent Heights/Laurel Canyon Boulevard, and continue eastward on Hollywood Boulevard, as it runs along the base of the Hollywood Hills.

Is this really *Hollywood Boulevard?* Isn't that famous street lined with movie theaters, restaurants, and shops? Yes, it is, but only in the section east of La Brea Avenue. In the one mile between Laurel Canyon and La Brea Avenue, Hollywood Boulevard is an attractive mixture of houses and apartment buildings, with the houses more prevalent in the blocks closest to Laurel Canyon.

On the left, opposite the head of Laurel Avenue, notice a splendidly landscaped Islamic-style house, complete with ever-so-exotic pointed windows and an eight-sided chimney.

Two blocks east of Fairfax Avenue, turn right on Ogden Avenue. Don't miss the Mayanesque **BOLLMAN RESIDENCE** at 1530 North Ogden, completed by Frank Lloyd Wright's eldest son, Lloyd, in 1922. According to Lloyd Wright, the steel-and-concrete-block construction of the Bollman house inspired his father to invent the textile-block technology, which was first used at the John Storer residence in 1923.

Don't overlook the Bollman house's neighbors. Where else but in Hollywood would you find a concrete Mayanesque home with a frame "Dutch Colonial" on one side and a picturesque half-timbered Tudor structure on the other? The architectural potpourri isn't limited to these three houses. Between Hollywood and Sunset boulevards, Ogden Drive and Orange Grove Avenue represent such a cross section of 1920s and 1930s architectural styles that production crews frequently use these streets and some of the houses as locations on television shows and movies.

Return to Hollywood Boulevard and continue eastward one block beyond Ogden Drive, turn left on **NICHOLS CANYON,** a narrow two-lane road which first runs along the bottom of this chic and still-rural canyon, then climbs into the steep chaparral-covered hillsides high above the city. The views of city, canyon, and other hillsides are spectacular on a smogless day.

If you have the time and the curiosity, explore whatever twisting Nichols Canyon roads that take your fancy. Along the way, you will notice that the houses are a mixture of new and not-so-new, large and small, attractive and downright ugly, much like neighboring Laurel Canyon to the west. (See page 59 of the Hollywood Hills Driving Tour.) Nichols Canyon, however, is a generally fancier address than Laurel Canyon, but it usually lacks Laurel's intimate glens and often-dense trees and shrubs.

When you have seen enough of Nichols Canyon, retrace your route and return to Hollywood Boulevard. If you can't remember the way you came, you should be able to find Nichols Canyon Road, and then Hollywood Boulevard, by following the streets downhill to the canyon floor. If you have driven quite far up into the hills above Nichols Canyon, don't be surprised if you come to Mulholland Drive, which runs along the crest of the Santa Monica Mountains (known as the Hollywood Hills in this part of Los Angeles). In this situation, turn around and head downhill until you reach Nichols Canyon Road at the bottom of the canyon. Or you might have even wandered into Laurel Canyon, which occasionally connects with Nichols Canyon high in the hills. If this has happened, just follow Laurel Canyon Boulevard down to Hollywood Boulevard and drive eastward half a dozen blocks to the entrance of Nichols Canyon.

Several blocks east of Nichols Canyon, turn left on Curson Avenue. Drive uphill until you reach the gate for Wattles Park at 1850 North Curson on your right.

WATTLES PARK is one of the little-known sights of Hollywood. Its 49 acres are a source of endless delight for nature lovers, hikers, and picnickers. Griffith Park, of course, is more popular and much larger. Barnsdall Park boasts an important Frank Lloyd Wright house and the Municipal Art Gallery atop its hill. But the picturesquely rundown Wattles Park offers an almost rural tranquillity, thanks to so few visitors, and it has a great variety of topography and flora because it stretches all the way from Hollywood Boulevard to the top of the Hollywood Hills in a long, narrow corridor.

At the turn of the century, Omaha, Nebraska, businessman Gurdon Wattles bought this 49-acre property for a winter residence, which he named "Jualita." In 1905 architects Myron Hunt and Elmer Grey, who designed the Beverly Hills Hotel and Henry E. Huntington's estate in Pasadena, built a spacious Mission Revival-style mansion on a hillock near the southern end of the property, overlooking then-unpaved Hollywood Boulevard and the open fields of present-day Hollywood. To the south and below the Wattles mansion, Hunt and Grey planted a lawn and orchards. Behind the house, they laid out a terraced formal garden, an area for roses, and a Japanese landscape.

Even after he retired in 1922 and made Jualita his year-round residence, Gurdon Wattles wanted to share his appreciation of nature with others and he permitted the public to visit the gardens at his estate. In 1968, the City of Los Angeles acquired this property from the Wattles family, and despite funding shortages which have been worsened by the tax-cutting Proposition 13, the city has halted further serious deterioration of the park and started modest restoration efforts.

If you turn right after entering Wattles Park's Curson Avenue gate, you first pass the Japanese teahouse and garden, which was a recent gift to Los Angeles from Nagoya, its sister city in Japan. Below that lie the rundown but essentially unaltered Wattles mansion and the remains of the formal gardens.

If you turn left after walking into the park, you immediately enter the long "Mediterranean zone," which is shaded by several dozen mature date palms. At the top of the Mediterranean zone, you come to a simple Japanese gate. On the other side lies the upper Japanese garden and, beyond that, the native flora of the upper hillside, which ends at The Crest, an observation point 950 feet above sea level.

Return to your car. Drive down Curson Avenue to Hollywood Boulevard, where you turn left. Proceed one block east and turn left on Sierra Bonita Avenue. Head uphill one block and turn right on Franklin Avenue and head eastward. Why have you left Hollywood Boulevard which you followed eastward for the last half mile? Because Hollywood Boulevard no longer is the east-to-west street that is closest to the hills. Now Franklin Avenue provides that east-to-west axis from which you turn onto the north-to-south side streets and explore hillside sights.

Just after you have come onto Franklin Avenue, turn left on **VISTA STREET,** which quickly deadends in the hills. What an incredibly atmospheric spot: little-changed 1920s houses, large gardens, hardly an apartment building in sight.

Turn around and head down the hill to Franklin Avenue. Turn left again.

42

ARCHITECTURAL CONTRAST. As you come to the next street, which is Camino Palmero, slow down. To the left, notice two large houses, which remain from the days when mansions lined much of Franklin Avenue. To the right stand long rows of apartments and condominiums. If these buildings seem graceless, even oppressive while they are now new, can you imagine how tacky they will look when they are old and out of style?

At the next street, Fuller Avenue, turn left and drive up the hill two blocks to the battered gates where the street comes to a dead end. Have you ever studied a detailed map of Hollywood and wondered about that blank street-less space just above this portion of Franklin Avenue? The reason is ***RUNYON CANYON,*** which lies on the other side of the gates.

Formerly the Huntington Hartford Estate, Runyon Canyon is the last large undeveloped parcel in the Hollywood Hills, totaling 133 acres to be exact. For years, Runyon Canyon has been a real estate developer's nightmare or an environmentalist's dream, depending on your outlook. Developers have prepared several plans to build expensive homes on the site, only to be bitterly opposed by local residents and subsequently to be turned down by the city. At the same time, the antidevelopment forces have put forth their own proposals to acquire Runyon Canyon as a public park, which would form an important part of a suggested hiking trail from downtown Los Angeles across the Santa Monica Mountains to the Pacific Ocean.

While both sides battle over the fate of Runyon Canyon, some Angelenos visit this virtually untouched area for picnics and hiking. They are, however, trespassing on private property.

Return to Franklin Avenue and turn left. From this small hill, you can see most of downtown Hollywood, including the looming off-white Holiday Inn and the circular Capitol Records Building.

Cross La Brea Avenue, but make sure you stay on Franklin Avenue. Two blocks east of La Brea, turn left on Outpost Drive. If you liked Nichols Canyon, you'll love ***OUTPOST ESTATES,*** which is the most sensitively planned major canyon and hillside district in Hollywood, thanks to the original 1924 developer, Charles Toberman, who insisted that utilities be located underground, all roads follow the natural contours of the land, and all houses have Spanish-style plaster walls and tile roofs. Because of its considerable beauty and convenient location, "the Outpost" remains one of Hollywood's most sought-after communities, sort of a less pretentious version of Beverly Hills, with service entrances at some houses, tall privacy-giving hedges along the roads, and gardeners' and poolmen's trucks parked along the curb.

After exploring Outpost Estates, return to Outpost Drive and turn left on Franklin Avenue. What an incredible contrast between the Outpost's elegant streets and this particularly gritty portion of the Hollywood "flats" just outside its entrance.

Just east of Outpost Drive, look up to the hills. If you think that you see a Japanese palace, it's not your imagination. Nor have you spotted a movie set which will be gone tomorrow. This is the Yamashiro Restaurant, and it is a real Japanese palace, at least "real" by Hollywood standards. For a closer look, turn left on Sycamore Avenue and follow this curving road up the hill, past the Magic Castle (which is a private club for magicians) until you reach the restaurant.

YAMASHIRO RESTAURANT, *1999 North Sycamore Avenue. Open for lunch Monday–Friday, 11:30 A.M. to 3:00 P.M. Buffet/brunch Saturday–Sunday, 11:30 A.M. to 3:00 P.M. Dinner Monday–Thursday, 5:30 P.M. to 10:30 P.M.; Friday, 5:30 P.M. to 11:30 P.M.; Saturday, 5:00 P.M. to 11:30 P.M.; Sunday, 5:00 P.M. to 10:30 P.M. Telephone: 466-5125. Moderate. American Express, MasterCard, and VISA credit cards.*

Yamashiro's sprawling building was erected as a private residence in 1913 by Adolphe and Eugene Bernheimer, who were Oriental art importers. The Bernheimer Brothers furnished their mansion with Japanese art and turned the 12-acre grounds into terraced Japanese gardens, complete with moats, cascades, and waterfalls, and a 600-year-old pagoda standing beside a pond.

Having gone through various reincarnations since the Bernheimers, this fanciful mansion appropriately has become a Japanese restaurant named Yamashiro, which means "mountain palace" in Japanese. Don't miss this Hollywood landmark. You can wander through the beautifully maintained grounds, then eat your Japanese or American dinner on the heated outdoor terrace or inside the comfortable picture-windowed dining room overlooking the city. Arrive near sunset and you can watch seemingly millions of lights sparkle in the city below.

Now for the disappointing part about Yamashiro: The Japanese and American meals could be better. Some Hollywood residents bring their out-of-town friends to Yamashiro for a drink, then head elsewhere for dinner. But they're wrong, because food is only one part of a pleasant dining experience. Other Japanese restaurants may serve finer meals, that's true, but can they match Yamashiro for history, atmosphere, and view?

Return to Franklin Avenue. Turn left and head eastward.

If you want to see another of Frank Lloyd Wright's textile-block houses, turn left on Hillcrest Road. Proceed up the steep hill one block, turn right on Glencoe Way, and park your car on the north side of the street. The Frank Lloyd Wright-designed residence is located on the right, just beyond the bend in the road. But if you drive past the house, then look for a parking space, you will get caught in an incredibly cramped cul de sac.

The **SAMUEL FREEMAN RESIDENCE** at 1962 Glencoe Way is the last of the four textile-block houses to be built in Los Angeles. The living room, dining area, and kitchen are located on street level, and the two bedrooms on the floor below. This small house conveys a feeling of remoteness because it seems to grow out of its heavily planted hillside, with walls and a blank façade on the street and the terraces and numerous windows on the other side, looking down Highland Avenue.

Return to Franklin Avenue, turn left, and drive east.

At the next street, Highland Avenue, turn left. Drive carefully. Highland Avenue is a fast-moving street, which connects to the Hollywood Freeway. Once you turn onto Highland, get into the left lane. After Franklin Avenue, the next stoplight is Camrose. Turn left on Camrose, go one or two blocks, and park your car. What a charming spot; the land is flat and the streets are little more than one lane wide. Most of the houses are cottages, some dating back to the teens and 1920s.

Don't miss **HIGHTOWER ROAD,** which intersects Camrose

45

on the north. At the end of this several-hundred-foot-long cul de sac stands a tall, slender Bologna-inspired tower, which contains an elevator connecting the street with the cluster of houses on the steep hillside above. Take the elevator up, explore this almost-unknown residential enclave, then walk down the winding staircase to the street below.

If you want to see the Hollywood Bowl, whose grounds are open from July 1 to September 30, return to Highland Avenue, turn left, and follow the appropriate signs.

The **HOLLYWOOD BOWL** is one of Hollywood's best-known landmarks, and deservedly so. Situated in a 116-acre park, it is a 17,000-seat natural amphitheater, and it has been the setting for outdoor musical performances since 1919. Today, the Hollywood Bowl is the summer home of the Los Angeles Philharmonic, which holds its "Symphonies Under the Stars" program from July 1 to September 30, but other musicians and singers appear here as well. The Hollywood Bowl also is the setting for an Easter sunrise service and a Fourth of July fireworks spectacular.

Having a good time at the Hollywood Bowl does require some planning. Parking is scarce, but you can find plenty of spaces in nearby lots along Highland Avenue. Or you may want to take one of the round-trip park-and-ride buses from a dozen different locations throughout Los Angeles.

Wherever you park, you must walk quite a way to reach your seat. Wear comfortable shoes. And bring a jacket or sweater, regardless of the late afternoon temperatures. Once the sun goes down, the Hollywood Hills usually cool off quickly, and you won't enjoy the music if your teeth are chattering. Should you be prone to fanny fatigue, bring a seat cushion or rent one at the Bowl, because the wooden bleacher-style seats can seem very hard after an hour or two.

Many people eat a picnic dinner at the Hollywood Bowl before performances. If you want to find a pleasant spot in the surrounding park, bring a blanket and arrive between 6:00 P.M. and 7:00 P.M. Or you can eat dinner at your seat. Don't forget to bring beer or wine.

Last but not least: Although the Hollywood Bowl has a sound

LEFT: *Japanese gardens at Yamashiro in the Hollywood Hills.*

ıHT: *Wattles Park in the Hollywood Hills.*

TOP LEFT: *Typical older Laurel Canyon house with typically laid-back dog.* TOP RIGHT: *A rustic street in Beachwood Canyon with the* HOLLYWOOD *sign standing in the background.* BOTTOM: *Vast stretches of the Hollywood Hills are undeveloped, such as this brush and wildflower-covered hillside overlooking the Lake Hollywood reservoir. The Hollywood flats and the rest of Los Angeles lie far beyond and hundreds of feet below the dam.*

TOP: *Entrance and garden at the Chateau Marmont Hotel, 8221 Sunset Boulevard.*
BOTTOM: *Sunset Strip billboard with the Art Deco Sunset Tower in the background.*

TOP LEFT: *Reflection of a "cut-out" billboard on a wall near the Sunset Strip.* TOP RIGHT: *Nymphs at play at International Terra Cotta on Robertson Boulevard.* BOTTOM: *The Tail O' The Pup, at the northwest corner of Beverly Boulevard and La Cienega Avenue, is better known for its "symbolic architecture"—it looks like a giant hot dog in a bun—than for its hot dogs.*

amplification system, don't expect concert-hall acoustics, particularly in the upper bleachers farthest from the stage. Select your programs carefully. The sound is best for symphonies, and the Hollywood Bowl is made for the *1812 Overture.* For concert information, call 876-8742.

Having seen the Hollywood Bowl, drive south on Highland Avenue. Turn left on Milner Street, which has a stoplight and is located directly opposite Camrose. If you decided to skip the Hollywood Bowl after seeing Hightower Road—and the Bowl isn't really that exciting except at concert time—just drive down Camrose, cross Highland Avenue, and drive up Milner Street on the opposite side.

On your left, notice the **CECIL B. DeMILLE BARN STUDIO,** at 2300 Highland Avenue, between Odin Street and Milner Road. If any single building symbolizes Hollywood's earliest years as the motion picture capital, it is this two-story frame barn, which originally stood at the southeast corner of Selma Avenue and Vine Street. Just before Christmas 1913, Cecil B. DeMille rented this barn for the Jesse L. Lasky Feature Play Company. A struggling stage-actor-turned-movie-director, the thirty-two-year-old DeMille had arrived in Hollywood from New York City with cameraman Alfredo Gandolfi, experienced director Oscar Apfel, and Broadway stage star Dustin Farnum to make a movie called *The Squaw Man.*

This faded yellow barn would be DeMille's studio. Actually, his tiny production company didn't get to use the entire building, because owner Harry Revier still kept his horse and carriage in one corner. Actors changed their clothes in empty horse stalls, and DeMille put his feet in the wastepaper basket under his desk whenever Revier washed the carriage and flooded the barn floor.

Although DeMille did not make the first movie in Hollywood, his makeshift barn studio quickly became known as the place "where 'Hollywood' was born." When *The Squaw Man* was released in February 1914, it became one of the movie industry's first nationwide box-office hits, grossing $225,000 on a production that cost $15,000.

Within several years of the film's release, the Famous Players

Company (later part of Paramount Pictures) had taken over the two blocks surrounding the DeMille barn. When Paramount shifted its operations to a 26-acre studio at Melrose Avenue and Marathon Street, several miles to the southeast, the barn was moved to the new location, where it became the company library, later the gymnasium, and finally part of the Wild West set. With the addition of a porch, the barn served as a set on the television series "Bonanza" in the 1960s.

In October 1979, Paramount gave the barn to the Hollywood Historic Trust, a part of the Hollywood Chamber of Commerce, and after yet another move, the rundown structure sat in a parking lot on Vine Street north of Hollywood Boulevard. Late in 1982, the Hollywood Historic Trust finally found a permanent home for the DeMille barn studio across from the Hollywood Bowl, where this landmark will be restored and opened as a small museum about silent-era film making. A print of *The Squaw Man* and one of the cameras used in making the film will be part of the exhibits. For information, dial UP-4-BARN (874-2276).

Follow Milner Road up the hill into **WHITLEY HEIGHTS,** a remarkable enclave of largely unchanged 1920s houses, situated on an elevated "triangle" bounded by Highland Avenue, Franklin Avenue, and the Hollywood Freeway. In 1982, Whitley Heights became a National Historic District, the first Hollywood neighborhood to be honored in this way by the Department of the Interior's National Register of Historic Places.

Just what makes Whitley Heights such an extraordinary spot? First, when J. J. Whitley developed this hillside in the late teens and 1920s, he specified that the houses have a Mediterranean feeling. Whitley, for instance, had sent his architect, Arthur Barnes, to northern Italy so that he could study the local building traditions. Second, Whitley carefully planned the community. The original houses were located so that they did not obscure their neighbors' views. Public stairs, moreover, connected each street with the ones above and below so that pedestrians didn't have to walk in the roads.

Third, an astonishing number of Hollywood celebrities have lived in Whitley Heights, including the costume designer Adrian,

Maurice Chevalier, Cecil B. DeMille, Marie Dressler, Janet Gaynor, Carmen Miranda, Tyrone Power, Rosalind Russell, Gloria Swanson, and Danny Thomas. Another famous resident was Rudolph Valentino, who bought a home at 6776 Wedgwood Place, on the east side of Whitley Heights, when he became a star in the early 1920s. This house was demolished for the Hollywood Freeway in 1949. Bette Davis' first home, which was a thatched-roof cottage with "spiderweb windows," originally stood toward the bottom of Whitley Heights' western flank, but it was torn down in 1962 for a Hollywood Museum, which was never built. The parking lots along Highland Avenue, north of Milner Road, occupy that site.

To see Whitley Heights, continue up Milner Road. When you reach a Y-shaped intersection with Watsonia Terrace, keep right along Milner. At the T-shaped intersection with Whitley Terrace, turn right and take this street around the hillside to Whitley Avenue. If you want to see more of Whitley Heights, park your car here and explore the rest of the neighborhood on foot. Otherwise, follow Whitley Avenue to the bottom of the steep hill, turn left on Franklin Avenue, and head east.

Just after the underpass beneath the Hollywood Freeway, notice the late 1920s Castle Argyle Apartments on the left northwest corner of Franklin and Argyle avenues. This is the *SITE OF CASTLE SANS SOUCI.*

During the teens, the grandest homes in Hollywood belonged not to newly arrived movie stars but to rich eccentrics like Alfred Guido Randolph Schloesser, a surgeon who made his fortune in mining. In 1912, Schloesser uprooted a lemon grove and built Castle Sans Souci, complete with leaded glass windows, crenellated rooflines, and a several-story tower. When virulent anti-German sentiment swept the United States during the First World War, the ever-ingenious Schloesser found an easy way out of his then-unfashionable last name: He simply switched names with his house. Schloesser became Alfred Guido Randolph Castle and Castle Sans Souci became Schloesser Terrace. Honest.

At the next street, Vista del Mar, turn left and drive up into the hills. Just beyond the long, rambling Goldwater Vista Villa Apartments on your right—now that's ugly!—park your car. Find 2130 Vista del Mar, the former **KRATONA COURT** Apartments, presently the Goldwater Patio Villas. Step through the entrance into the central courtyard. Look up straight ahead. See the Islamic-style dome? Do you notice the horseshoe-shaped doorways near you? This time, the reason for this outrageous architecture is not 1920s eclecticism. Instead, it is the religious cult that built these apartments.

New or unusual religious beliefs are nothing new in Los Angeles. In 1913 Alfred Powell Warrington, a Norfolk, Virginia, attorney-turned-Hollywood guru, founded a 15-acre Theosophical retreat named Kratona in the Hollywood Hills, just east of the present-day Hollywood Freeway. Warrington believed that man could establish direct mystical contact with divine principles through contemplation, and he selected the Hollywood Hills for Kratona, in his words, because "a spiritual urge seems to be peculiar to all this section" and "the prevailing breezes from off the nearby Pacific Ocean give physical tone to the surroundings." Warrington also reported that the Hollywood Hills were "magnetically impregnated."

When hundreds of true believers flocked to Kratona in the mid-teens, Warrington erected several apartment buildings—including this one, a Moorish-style occult temple, a psychic lotus pond, a vegetarian cafeteria, and a metaphysical library. Kratona became so popular that Warrington rented a hall on Hollywood Boulevard to teach courses in Esperanto, the Esoteric Interpretation of Music and Drama, and the human aura.

During the 1930s, the Kratona cult lost many of its followers, and it moved to Ojai, north of Los Angeles. Since then, Kratona's temple, cafeteria, and library have vanished, but you can still find the rundown former Kratona Court on this hillside. Do not disturb the occupants.

Return to Franklin Avenue and turn left. Two blocks ahead, you pass **BEACHWOOD CANYON,** which is described on page 68 of the Hollywood Hills Driving Tour.

Continue eastward on Franklin Avenue until you reach Western Avenue, a major north-to-south thoroughfare. Turn left on

Western, proceed uphill, then follow the curve to the right onto Los Feliz Boulevard, one of the most majestic-looking streets in Los Angeles, thanks to the deep front lawns, mature trees, and largely Spanish-style mansions on both sides.

Just beyond this curve, get into the left lane, then turn left at the first stoplight onto Fern Dell, which is one of the entrances to **GRIFFITH PARK.** You can also drive into Griffith Park from Vermont Avenue, which intersects Los Feliz Boulevard one mile to the east. To enter Griffith Park by car, you must pay fifty cents Monday to Friday and $1.00 Saturday and Sunday, when it is far more crowded. For this fee, you can get a simple but useful map of the park. Griffith Park is open from 5:30 A.M. to 10:30 P.M., except the mountain roads which close at sunset. For information, call 665-5188.

Griffith Park is the nation's largest municipal park, totaling 4, 063 acres in all. Because of its enormous size and varied topography, it is many parks in one, suited to all kinds of activities. In the flatlands, which tend to be located around the north, east, and south periphery, Griffith Park offers golf courses, tennis courts, soccer fields, riding stables where you can rent horses, and baseball fields, as well as merry-go-rounds, a miniature train ride, a bird sanctuary, a pony ring, and a zoo. Most of Griffith Park, however, is often-rugged hillsides and canyons, crisscrossed by hiking and riding trails. If you would rather enjoy this undeveloped land from a moving car, take Western Canyon Road, which leads off from Fern Dell.

Of course, the best-known feature of Griffith Park is the Observatory, which can be approached by car from the Fern Dell or Vermont Avenue entrances. Just follow the signs. Located on a mountainside facing south, the Griffith Observatory's massive stone walls and green copper dome can be seen from almost anywhere in the Hollywood flats. The view of Los Angeles is outstanding, smog willing. Even without the views, Griffith Observatory offers something for everyone: fascinating science exhibits, astronomical shows in the Planetarium Theater, and the Laserium light and music shows. For Observatory information, call 664-1191; for Laserium information, call 997-3624.

Griffith Park marks the end of the Lower Hollywood Hills Tour. To return to the Hollywood "flats" or major east-to-west thoroughfares like Sunset or Santa Monica boulevards, leave Griffith Park and drive south on Western or Vermont avenues.

6
Upper Hollywood Hills Driving Tour

BACKGROUND

If any single topographical feature symbolizes Los Angeles, it is the Santa Monica Mountains, which start near the downtown and run 15 miles westward to the Pacific Ocean. Known as the Hollywood Hills in their several-mile passage through Hollywood, these mountains provide a dramatic backdrop for such well-known landmarks as the HOLLYWOOD sign and the Griffith Observatory, and they divide the sprawling city into Los Angeles proper on the coastal plain and the inland San Fernando Valley.

For affluent Angelenos, the canyons and the hillsides of the still reasonably undeveloped Hollywood Hills offer quiet, pretty, almost-rustic places to live, usually no more than a ten-minute drive from shops and offices in the flats. For residents of the densely populated Hollywood flats or West Hollywood, the Hollywood Hills provide plenty of open space for outdoor gatherings, to hike through, or simply to look at.

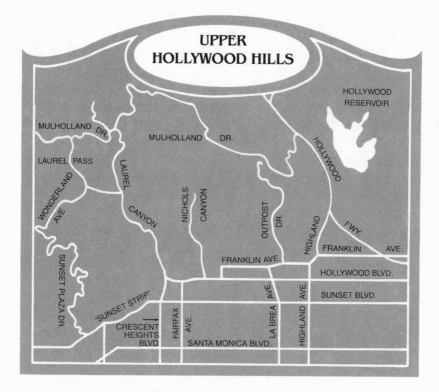

Despite their inescapable physical presence, much of the Hollywood Hills remains something of a mystery to tourists and many Angelenos. Some roads dead-end after a mile or two. Others lead into heavily developed canyons that look like suburbia-gone-country. And many of the best architectural, natural, or topographical sights are frustratingly difficult to find, even if you know about them.

The following Hollywood Hills Driving Tour includes many of the most interesting sights, and it is divided into western, central, and eastern portions so that you can end your drive one-third or two-thirds of the way through and return to the flats. Don't shortchange yourself by doing this. The entire tour requires about three hours, with plenty of time allowed for stops, and when you have finished, you will know the Hollywood Hills better than many lifelong Angelenos.

54

HOLLYWOOD HILLS DRIVING TOUR   *Western Portion of the Hollywood Hills and Laurel Canyon.*
TIME: *One hour, without extensive stops.*

Start at the intersection of Sunset Boulevard and Sunset Plaza Drive, which is one mile west of Crescent Heights Boulevard.

Turn right on Sunset Plaza Drive and head up into the westernmost reaches of the Hollywood Hills, which are part of the Santa Monica Mountains chain. A little less than a mile west of Sunset Plaza, these hills pass through the upper reaches of Beverly Hills, then Bel Air, then Brentwood, and finally Pacific Palisades and Malibu, which overlook the Pacific Ocean.

Immediately after you turn onto Sunset Plaza Drive and pass the Greek templelike John La Joie beauty salon on the right, but before the first left turn, you see a stand of mature windmill palms on the right. These medium-size fan-leafed palms are a favorite street and garden tree in Los Angeles.

Just beyond the first left curve, and on the left side of the road, is a 10-foot-high Canary Island date palm. This particular tree is about twenty years old, and its bushy head of foliage already is fully developed. Soon, the thick trunk will start growing, and eventually it will reach a height of 60 feet, but the bushy top will remain the same size as it rises higher and higher into the air.

For the first half mile, Sunset Plaza Drive passes dozens of Regency-esque and Colonial Revival-style houses of the 1930s and 1940s. While none of these residences is an architectural landmark, most are attractive looking, properly situated on the hillsides, and handsomely landscaped with mature trees and shrubs. Seen all together, these houses form an appealing streetscape, which looks like it could be located in one of the older commuter towns of Westchester County, New York, or on Chicago's North Shore, except for the palm trees and the year-round flower gardens.

As you drive farther up the hill, be sure to follow the signs for Sunset Plaza Drive. Don't turn onto Sunset Plaza Terrace or Sunset Plaza Place by mistake.

55

On the right, notice 1670 Sunset Plaza Drive, which was designed by John Lloyd Wright, one of Frank Lloyd Wright's sons. John's buildings are rare, because he was not as prolific as his father or his older brother, Frank Lloyd, Jr., who practiced under the name Lloyd Wright. But you can easily see a certain family resemblance in this house's precast concrete-block appliqué, which Frank Lloyd Wright introduced in a different form on his Los Angeles textile-block houses in the early 1920s.

As you proceed farther up Sunset Plaza Drive the land becomes steeper and the building lots smaller and more irregular. Rather than the large traditional-looking 1930s and 1940s residences, which are found just above Sunset Boulevard, the houses usually are modern stucco boxes, which are perched on hillsides or rest on stilts. In contrast to the older houses which fit into the landscape gracefully, these newer structures stand in solitary splendor on minimally landscaped, often barren hillsides, as if the panoramic view from the picture windows is the only thing that matters. Ranging in style from mock-Tudor to Taco-Bell Spanish, these new houses blight all parts of the Hollywood Hills, not just Sunset Plaza Drive, and they reflect real estate developers' greed and insensitivity in this dramatic setting, which deserves better architecture.

Just before you reach 1847 Sunset Plaza Drive, which is on your left, you will see what appears to be a cement hillside on your right. This is gunnite, a cementlike material which is sprayed directly on the hills in order to prevent erosion that can topple houses from their mountaintops.

This gunnite hillside is particularly offfensive because it has been left its natural gray color, which does not blend into the landscape as well as brown-tinted material would. Of course, using deeply rooted plants is an aesthetically and environmentally preferable method of erosion control. But most architects and developers opt for gunnite, because suitable plants take years to sink their roots into the ground and, even then, they cannot stabilize the hillsides which probably should not have been built upon in the first place.

Why does this particular gunnite wall have so many little holes on its surface? So that rain water can seep out of the hill.

Otherwise it would collect in winter storms and quickly fracture the thin cementlike wall.

Just beyond 1905 Sunset Plaza Drive, on your left, you see a stand of feathery-leafed acacia, the hardy evergreen shrub and tree that was introduced to the West Coast in the 1850s and has become so common that many Californians assume that it is a native plant. Although acacias come in hundreds of different species, only about twenty are found in California. Many of these species bloom in January or February, turning into a mass of small gold flowers, which are often quite fragrant. Except for its twenty- to thirty-year lifespan, the acacia is the perfect all-around tree for coastal Southern California. It is hardy, drought-resistant, and grows rapidly, sometimes twenty feet in just three years.

On the hillside to the right, notice the castor bean plant, a summer annual which actually turns into a tall and leafy shrub in the mild Southern California climate. The castor bean produces small white flowers in early spring, and later in the year it yields prickly surfaced pods which contain the shining mottled beans. The plants are grown commercially for—you guessed it—castor oil, which comes from the beans. Caution: The beans are poisonous, and some people are allergic to contact with the leaves and beans.

In the space between 1917 and 1923 Sunset Plaza Drive, look at the other side of the canyon and see the tennis court that has been cantilevered over the hillside. What an expensive way to play tennis.

Below the tennis court are four cantilevered contemporary houses, designed by Richard Banta, who was one of the first architects to develop stilt housing in the hills. The house on the left, which was completed first and built with steel supports, is architecturally pleasing and earthquake-resistant. The three other houses follow a standard plan that Banta worked out for hillside development.

While you are parked, notice the laurel sumac, a six- to fifteen-foot California native, which has several-inch-long light green laurel-like leaves and small off-white flowers that bloom in the early summer. This shrub is well-chosen for the barren parts

57

of the Hollywood Hills, because it controls erosion and is very drought-resistant, a plus in Los Angeles' rainless summers and falls. Laurel sumac is related to poison oak and poison sumac, but it does not cause a skin rash. Yet, it does have one disagreeable quality—the leaves stink if they are crushed.

Keep driving higher and higher into the hills until Sunset Plaza Drive ends at the intersection of Crescent and Wonderland avenues, which is 2.8 miles from Sunset Boulevard. You have reached one of the highest spots in the Hollywood Hills. Park your car along one of the almost traffic-free roads and look down on Los Angeles' urban sprawl that has obliterated the ranches, orange groves, and scattered communities which filled this coastal plain at the turn of the century.

On clear days, which are more common in winter and spring than during the summer and fall, you can see about as far east as the Los Angeles County Museum of Art on Wilshire Boulevard, just east of Fairfax Avenue. The hills, however, block the view of the rapidly growing downtown Los Angeles skyline. To the south, you can see the Palos Verdes peninsula, a fashionable countrified suburb since the 1920s which rises high above the Pacific Ocean, and beyond that the largely unsettled Catalina Island, which is 27 miles offshore yet still a part of Los Angeles County. To the west, the view includes Santa Monica and the endless expanse of the Pacific Ocean.

If you carefully study the portion of the city immediately below, you will notice a line where the dull browns and grays of the city end and a much greener section begins. This is Doheny Drive, the north-south boundary between West Hollywood, which is part of Los Angeles, and Beverly Hills, which is an independent municipality of 32,000 residents.

From this mountaintop vantage point, you can see how sensitive city planning, not to mention lots of money, dramatically affects the quality of urban life, because the green in Beverly Hills is street trees. In Los Angeles, some streets have trees along the curbs, while others do not. Usually, the presence of street trees depends on the generosity of the neighborhood's original developer or the residents' subsequent efforts to improve their block. But trees require regular care, and Los Angeles' efforts are casual at best, thanks to the city and county's severe fiscal crunch since the passage of tax-cutting Proposition 13. In contrast, Beverly Hills has a street tree master plan which specifies that a certain species be planted along the length of every street, and the city government stil has the funds to maintain the trees properly, even if that means raising a man 40 to 50 feet into the air in a cherrypicker in order to trim the palms.

Before returning to your car for the drive through Laurel Canyon, admire the line of eucalyptus trees along unpaved Wonderland Avenue. The eucalyptus is another mid-nineteenth-century import from Australia, and it probably is the most common non-native tree in California, because it is attractive, drought-resistant, pest-free, and fast-growing, sometimes up to 10 feet in a year at the beginning. Unlike most other quick-growing trees, the properly situated eucalyptus can live a hundred years, even more. When several eucalyptus trees stand together, they give off a wonderful fragrance, and their flat leaves produce a delightful rustling sound in the wind.

At the base of the third eucalyptus tree along Wonderland Avenue, don't miss the Christmasberry bush, a California native with long dark-green serrated leaves. In midsummer, this evergreen shrub produces clusters of small white flowers, which are followed by bright red berries in winter, hence its name.

Farther ahead, between the fifth and sixth trees, you will see the wild cucumber plant. This hardy vine grows from a huge root which is as big around as a man's thigh and sits buried deep in the ground. In spring, this plant has white flowers, and later in the year, it produces a bad-tasting cucumber.

On your way back to the car, you will pass a wooden fence on the left. Look down. In the steep backyard of the modern stucco house, you will see the coast live oak, another native species to California which frequently grows as high as 60 or 70 feet in the canyons scattered throughout the Santa Monica Mountains. With its thick foliage of one- to three-inch leaves, the live oak also makes a fine 10- to 15-foot hedge.

For the secret back entrance to Laurel Canyon, drive down Wonderland Avenue. Don't be alarmed that the street is unpaved. Using caution and good brakes, even the most softly sprung American automobile can navigate this road. Besides, the unpaved stretch of Wonderand Avenue lasts only a tenth of a mile.

Laurel Canyon is one of those spots which make Los Angeles such a comfortable place to live. Settled around the turn of the century, it probably is the most rustic canyon within the city limits, thanks to the many steep hillsides which are prohibitively expensive for large-scale development. Consequently, Laurel Canyon abounds in birds and small animals, including the mischievous coyote, and in many places the trees and shrubs come up to the edge of the narrow winding roads, thereby hiding quite a few houses from view.

Driving down Wonderland Avenue, you see the variety of housing in Laurel Canyon, indeed in much of the Hollywood Hills, which ranges from the picturesquely rundown early twentieth-century cabin to the pretentious new Beverly Hills-style gated estate. Don't miss the quaint-looking 8964 Wonderland Avenue, one of Laurel Canyon's earliest houses, which is nestled in the hillside and shaded by a live oak.

Follow Wonderland Avenue all the way down the hill to Laurel Pass Avenue, where you see a school on the right. Turn left and drive up Laurel Pass through an early 1960s subdivision named Laurel Hills.

At the second STOP sign, which is one mile after you started up Laurel Pass, turn right on the winding two-lane-wide Mulholland Drive, which runs along the crest of the Santa Monica Mountains and offers breathtaking views of chaparral-covered hillsides and Los Angeles on one side and the flat expanse of the San Fernando Valley on the other. Although the San Fernando Valley is more dramatic-looking at night because of the several million lights, avoid this section of Mulholland Drive on Friday and Saturday evenings, unless that is the only time that you have available. On some weekend nights, drag racers take over this stretch of the highway between Coldwater and Laurel canyons, unless the police set up roadblocks and patrol the road with searchlight-equipped helicopters. Either way, it is not a pleasant place to visit.

Just after turning onto Mulholland Drive, you will see a large roadside plant, which has several-foot-long dark-green spiky leaves with yellow edges. This is the somewhat misleadingly named century plant, which grows for ten to twenty years, then sends up a thick 15- to 20-foot stem that eventually produces yellow-green flowers. Once this flowering is complete—and it literally can take several years—the century plant dies, although sucker plants usually sprout nearby. The imposing flower stem remains standing until it dries out and falls over in the wind, usually in a few years' time.

Just beyond the century plant, you will reach the entrance to Laurel Canyon Park on the right. Nestled in the hills, this small park is quiet, clean, secluded, and little used, and it is the perfect place to stretch your legs or eat a picnic lunch at one of the tables. Open from 6:00 A.M. to 8:00 P.M..

Upon leaving the park, turn right on Mulholland Drive. When you reach the stoplight at the busy intersection of Mulholland Drive and Laurel Canyon Boulevard, which is one of the few routes over the Hollywood Hills from Los Angeles to the San Fernando Valley, you have completed the western portion of the Hollywood Hills Tour. If you want to end your drive at this point, turn right on Laurel Canyon Boulevard, which leads down through Laurel Canyon, until you reach Sunset and Crescent Heights boulevards in the flatlands. Or you may continue straight ahead on Mulholland Drive into the central portion of the Hollywood Hills. The remaining central and eastern portions of the Hollywood Hills Tour go more quickly than the western section.

HOLLYWOOD HILLS DRIVING TOUR   *Central Portion.*
TIME: *Thirty minutes.*

After you cross Laurel Canyon Boulevard, stay on Mulholland Drive past occasional houses, brush-covered or barren hillsides, and glimpses of the San Fernando Valley to the left. In about one mile, you will see a turnout on your left. Watch for oncoming traffic, cross over the dividing line, and park your car.

61

From this lofty spot, you can see most of the 22-mile-long San Fernando Valley, popularly known as "The Valley," which is separated from Los Angeles proper and the coastal plain by the Santa Monica Mountains, which you are driving along. On the opposite side of the San Fernando Valley, you see the San Gabriel and Santa Susana Mountains, which form the other boundary of The Valley and separate it from the hot Central Valley.

Throughout the late nineteenth century, and particularly after the introduction of water from the distant Owens Valley in 1913, the San Fernando Valley was filled with orange groves, barley fields, and cattle ranches, plus occasional villages and housing tracts which were linked to Los Angeles by the Pacific Electric Railroad. In the 1920s and 1930s, the San Fernando Valley started to become a suburban extension of Los Angeles as families spilled over the Santa Monica Mountains in search of reasonably priced single-family houses and large yards to call their own.

At first, suburban growth was concentrated in the eastern end of the San Fernando Valley, in towns like Glendale and Burbank, which are north of downtown Los Angeles, and in communities like North Hollywood or Studio City, which were accessible to Hollywood and the rest of Los Angeles through the Cahuenga Pass over the Hollywood Hills.

After the Second World War, the San Fernando Valley experienced a massive population and building boom, which was partly made possible by the construction of limited-access, high-speed freeways, beginning with the Arroyo Seco Parkway, which opened between Los Angeles and Pasadena in 1942. Single-family housing tracts and shopping centers steadily moved westward across the San Fernando Valley, through Van Nuys, Reseda, and Canoga Park, to name a few communities. Today, the Valley has over a million residents, and it accounts for one-third of Los Angeles' total population.

Although hillside areas in Sherman Oaks, Encino, and Woodland Hills are definitely upper middle class and affluent, most of the San Fernando Valley is decidedly middle class and about 75 percent white. As such, The Valley is the object of derision and more than a little contempt by some Hollywood or Beverly Hills residents who consider themselves to be more sophisticated and better educated, much the same as Manhattanites look down on Queens or Long Island residents.

Whatever San Fernando Valley residents are really like, this vast 177-square-mile part of Los Angeles no longer fits the suburban stereotype of one housing tract after another. To the east or your far right from this turnout, heavy industry is located in San Fernando, Sylmar, and Pacoima. Office buildings have sprouted throughout the San Fernando Valley, especially where major freeways come together, such as the North Hollywood/ Studio City/Universal City area at the intersection of the Holly-wood and Ventura freeways to the right or Sherman Oaks at the intersection of the San Diego and Ventura freeways to the far left. And the single-family house no longer dominates the hous-ing market exclusively. Because of lofty real estate prices, more and more Valley residents live in apartments and condominiums strung out along the major boulevards or located in virtually self-contained enclaves.

After leaving the turnout, you will pass 7820 Mulholland Drive, which was designed by Richard Neutra, the Vienna-born architect who came to Los Angeles in 1925. A gifted practitioner of the International style, Neutra successfuly applied modern technology to house construction, and he was the ideal architect for Los Angeles' dramatic hillsides, because he believed that buildings should complement, not overwhelm their natural settings.

Just beyond the Neutra-designed house, you pass Torreyson Place. Continue a few hundred feet more along Mulholland Drive, then pull your car over to the side, and look to your right and somewhat to the rear. The Malin Chemosphere house rises from the hillside like a giant mushroom. Actually, the Chem-osphere house is an eight-sided saucer that sits on a single concrete post, which was architect John Lautner's highly origi-nal—and dramatic—way of using this striking location without bulldozing the hillside in order to provide enough flat space for a conventionally designed dwelling. And who would ever guess that residents reach the house by way of a tram that runs from

63

the garage area at the bottom of the hill to the front door several hundred feet above?

On your right, the rambling Colonial-style house is Errol Flynn's "Mulholland House," which was the scene of the gambling, drinking, and whoring that the actor so vividly described in his autobiography *My Wicked, Wicked Ways*. The house also was a crash pad for many of Flynn's friends, such as actor John Barrymore, who stayed here often in the late 1930s when he was fighting with his wife and drinking more heavily than ever.

In *My Wicked, Wicked Ways*, Flynn tells how he awoke one evening to hear Barrymore screaming, "Let me out, you bastard, let me out! Flynn, you traitor, let me out of here!" Running down the hall to the guest room, Flynn discovered that Barrymore had gotten out of bed to go to the bathroom but was so drunk that he had walked into the closet instead. By the time Flynn reached the room, Barrymore was pounding on the closet walls, shouting, "Bats! Your house is full of bats!" While wandering around the closet looking for the toilet, he had backed into some coat hangers and felt a ticklish "batlike" sensation on the neck. None of this would have ever happened if Barrymore had followed his usual practice of urinating out the window.

Just past the intersection of Mulholland and Woodrow Wilson drives, you see a mammoth pink structure on the hillside straight ahead. This is Rudy Vallee's tennis court, complete with a huge ballroom underneath, where the aging singer stores all the memorabilia from his career. On top of the hill, Vallee lives in a pink stucco 1920s Spanish-style villa, which has breaktaking 360-degree views of Los Angeles and the San Fernando Valley.

Rudy Vallee's street address is Pyramid Place. Several years ago, he asked the City Council to change the name to Rue de Vallee. Get it? Some of his neighbors objected and the name remains Pyramid Place.

Just beyond 7456 Mulholland Drive, you come to a small turnout on the right, where you can see much of Nichols Canyon, which is less rustic but more fashionable than Laurel Canyon to the west.

After you pass Pyramid Place, you can look down on the Hollywood Freeway and Central Hollywood, including the circular

Capitol Records Building, which resembles an enormous stack of phonograph records, topped by a 20-foot-high styluslike chimney.

Farther on, the HOLLYWOOD sign and the domed Griffith Observatory sit on distant hillsides straight ahead. Down below and much closer, you can see Cahuenga Pass, which takes its name from the Cahuenga Indians who lived in Hollywood before the arrival of the Spanish and Mexican settlers in the eighteenth century. Cahuenga Pass was the easiest route over this portion of the Santa Monica Mountains, and therefore it became part of El Camino Real, the Spanish highway which ran up the California coast from mission to mission. Until the arrival of the railroad in 1876, the Camino Real was Los Angeles' major link to the rest of California and the nation. Since 1954, Cahuenga Pass has been part of the Hollywood Freeway.

When you drive down a hill above the Hollywood Freeway, you come to an old cement bridge which crosses the highway. Turn right and follow the bridge until you reach the STOP sign on the other end. Turn left on Lake Ridge Place.

At this point, you have come to the end of the tour through the central portion of the Hollywood Hills. You may conclude your drive by heading down Lake Ridge Place until you reach Barham Boulevard, which has an entrance to the Hollywood Freeway that leads to the San Fernando Valley to the north or back to Hollywood and Los Angeles to the south.

HOLLYWOOD HILLS DRIVING TOUR *Eastern Portion and Beachwood Canyon.*

TIME: *Thirty minutes.*

A few hundred feet after you turn onto Lake Ridge Place, you come to Wonder View Drive, which has a small unofficial street sign. Turn right on Wonder View Drive and proceed through a lovely undeveloped canyon. Can you identify the acacia, eucalyptus, and laurel sumac, having seen these trees earlier on this tour? Also, do you know why dirt tracks cut across the meadows and the hills? Motorcyclists and dirt-bikers come to this out-of-the-way spot and try to see how steep a hill they can climb, in the process scarring the landscape and disturbing the local residents who moved to this canyon because of its quiet and natural beauty.

When you drive up the first hill and reach a T intersection, turn right and continue along Wonder View Drive, thereby avoiding Tareco Drive. At the next intersection, which is Y-shaped, turn left and head up the hill to another T, where you turn right, still continuing along Wonder View. Follow these directions closely. Many of the street signs are missing, no doubt removed by local residents who want to discourage any more outsiders from finding their way into this Shangri-la setting.

At the next STOP sign, go around the ivy-planted traffic circle and continue straight ahead on Wonder View, past charming houses that look like they are located in some Middle Western town rather than on a mountain ridge in Southern California.

At the next STOP sign, turn right and stay on Wonder View, then make an immediate right on Lake Hollywood Drive. Now you see the Lake Hollywood Reservoir below, plus the dam built by engineer William Mulholland in the 1930s. This is the dam that supposedly broke in the movie *Earthquake*.

Outdoors buffs rejoice! Lake Hollywood is one of those peaceful places that most Los Angelenos don't know about, and if they do, they usually can't find it. At the bottom of the hill, you may park your car and hike or jog around the lake, which is a distance of 3.5 miles. The pedestrian gate is open weekdays from 6:30 A.M. to 10:00 A.M. and from 2:00 P.M. to 5:00 P.M., and on weekends it is open from 6:30 A.M. to 5:00 P.M..

After leaving the pedestrian gate, follow Lake Hollywood Drive around the eastern edge of the reservoir, past the brush-covered hillsides on the left and a row of Appian pines alongside the lake on the right. Who would ever guess that this secluded spot is in the middle of Los Angeles?

Just before Lake Hollywood Drive ends at another gate, turn left on Tahoe Drive. At the first STOP sign, turn right on Canyon Lake Drive. At the top of the hill, you reach a Y intersection. Turn left on Mulholland Highway.

If any single landmark symbolizes Hollywood, indeed all of Los Angeles, it is the HOLLYWOOD sign in the Hollywood Hills atop the chaparral-covered south side of Mt. Lee. Constructed in 1923 at a cost of $21,000, the sign originally read HOLLYWOOD-LAND, because it advertised a stylish 500-acre subdivision by that name in nearby Beachwood Canyon. Each of the thirteen letters was 30 feet wide and 50 feet high, and they were built of sheet metal that was secured to a scaffold of pipes, wires, and telephone poles. A line of 20-watt bulbs ran around each letter, one every eight inches, and on clear evenings, the HOLLYWOODLAND sign was visible for miles.

The sign also became an occasional jumping-off spot for suicides, beginning with young blond Peg Entwhistle. A British actress who had appeared in several Broadway plays, Peg came to Hollywood in hopes of becoming a movie star and stayed with her uncle who lived at 2428 Beachwood Drive. Peg got bit parts in several RKO films, but the studio did not renew its option on her contract in July 1932. Unable to find other work, Peg sat around her uncle's house and rode a horse in the hills beneath the HOLLYWOODLAND sign almost every day.

On Friday evening, September 16, 1932, Peg told her uncle that she was going out to buy a package of cigarettes. Instead, she climbed up Mt. Lee to the HOLLYWOODLAND sign and made her final exit from the giant H letter.

Following the Second World War, the Hollywood Chamber of Commerce removed the "LAND" from the hillside, but by the 1970s, the sign was falling apart. In 1978, the top half of the first O was missing, the third O was entirely gone, and the rest of the letters looked like a giant moth had nibbled their edges. The HOLLYWOOD sign's future looked bleak until *Playboy* publisher Hugh Hefner held a benefit party at the Playboy Mansion, which yielded $45,000 toward its reconstruction. Shortly thereafter, rock star Alice Cooper donated $27,700, which was the exact cost of rebuilding one letter in steel and concrete. Cooper selected the last O, which he dedicated to Groucho Marx. The idea of buying a letter quickly caught on. For $27,700, Gene Autry selected the second L. Andy Williams took the W. Warner Brothers Records paid for the second O, and so forth. On November

11, 1978, the new HOLLYWOOD sign was dedicated, while search-lights scanned the dark nighttime skies in true show business fashion.

While looking at the HOLLYWOOD sign, you probably have no-ticed the enormous Spanish-style mansion rising on a nearby hillside. This is Castillo del Lago, which was built by oil explorer Patrick Longan in 1926. This house, which some people simply call "The Castle," marches nine stories up this steep hillside, and it measures 106 feet from its front door to the top of its tower. Although Castillo del Lago has 20,000 square feet of space, only 8,000 are usable because of the house's towers and winding staircases.

During the 1930s, mobster Bugsey Siegel reportedly op-erated a gambling den in the mansion. Castillo del Lago fit Bugsey's security needs perfectly—or so he thought. The only entrance was through a courtyard near the bottom of the house at the end of a long, narrow, winding driveway. The police would never attack the house from this approach. Because of the house's unobstructed views, Bugsey's strong-arm men thought that they could see the police coming from all other directions. But they were wrong. One night the police stormed Castillo del Lago from the one neighboring house, and Bugsey's gambling-den days were over, at least for a while.

Shortly after you pass Castillo del Lago and drive alongside a steep barren hillside on your right, Mulholland Highway splits into a high road and a low road. Take either one to Ledgewood Drive and follow this street down the hill into Beachwood Can-yon. When Ledgewood reaches Beachwood Drive, turn right.

Take your time. Thanks to sensitively laid-out hillside streets and strict architectural controls when the Hollywoodland sub-division opened in 1923, Beachwood Canyon is one of the most charming residential areas in all Los Angeles today, and it abounds in scarcely changed 1920s and 1930s Spanish-style houses, plus a handful of equally handsome English cottages and would-be Norman castles.

If you are hungry—and want to see one place that movie and television personalities really do frequent—visit the lunch counter at the Beachwood Market at 2701 Belden Drive, just off Beachwood Drive.

Just beyond the market, you see the picturesque sandstone gates that mark the entrance to the Hollywoodland tract. Once you pass these gates, your Hollywood Hills driving tour is over. The neighborhood drops several economic notches at once, but it is still a good place to live, and many of the houses and apartment building are architectural gems. If you still feel adventuresome, explore any of the side streets to the right or left. Beachwood Drive ends at Franklin Avenue, a busy thoroughfare which offers easy access to the rest of Hollywood and Los Angeles.

7
The Sunset Strip

BACKGROUND

Probably it was Edd Byrnes who really put the Sunset Strip on the map. Between 1958 and 1962, Byrnes played a hair-combing parking attendant named Kookie on the "77 Sunset Strip" television series. Quickly becoming a teenage heartthrob, Byrnes stole much of the attention from "77 Sunset Strip" star Efrem Zimbalist, Jr., and boosted the show's ratings so high that millions of Americans learned that the Strip was synonymous with good times, fast women, and even faster cars. Remember, this was the Fifties.

The Sunset Strip is the 1.5-mile stretch of Sunset Boulevard that runs along the base of the Hollywood Hills between Crescent Heights Boulevard in West Hollywood and the eastern edge of Beverly Hills. By a quirk of municipal boundaries, the Sunset Strip is not a part of the City of Los Angeles. Instead it is located in a several-square-mile section of unincorporated Los Angeles

County, which is surrounded on all sides by the cities of Los Angeles and Beverly Hills.

As a part of the county, the Sunset Strip was free of some city-mandated laws, and during the 1930s it became the location of fashionable nightclubs, bars, and restaurants. The first of the posh nightclubs was the Trocadero Café, which opened at 8610 Sunset Boulevard in 1934 and quickly became a favorite with Angelenos, tourists, and occasional show business celebrities who wanted to dance, drink, and be entertained by stars like Deanna Durbin, Judy Garland, Mary Martin, or Martha Raye. Next came Ciro's at 8433 Sunset Boulevard, and over the years some of its best-known entertainers included Josephine Baker, Maurice Chevalier, Sammy Davis, Jr., Peggy Lee, Jerry Lewis and Dean Martin, and Sophie Tucker, as well as Eartha Kitt, who made her nightclub debut here. The third well-known Sunset Strip night spot was the Mocambo at 8588 Sunset Boulevard, and some of its most famous entertainers were Billy Daniels, Lena Horne, and Edith Piaf.

In addition to these nightclubs, the Sunset Strip's other must-see attraction was the Garden of Allah Hotel, which was named for Alla Nazimova, the Russian-born stage actress who started making silent pictures in the United States during the mid-teens. Nicknamed "the Woman of 1000 Moods," Nazimova built a Spanish-style mansion, complete with "moon parlor," at 8150 Sunset Boulevard in the early 1920s, and she planted the surrounding three-acre grounds with poplars, cedars, and fruit trees. Her swimming pool was shaped like the Black Sea.

When Nazimova's star waned in the late 1920s, she sold her estate to a real estate developer, who converted the mansion into a hotel and built 25 guest bungalows on the grounds. As part of the deal, Nazimova could also live in an apartment on the second floor of her former home for the remainder of her life. A star to the very end, Nazimova insisted that people address her as "Madame," and she hated the phrase "good night" because it meant bad luck.

Almost immediately after opening in 1927, the Garden of Allah became a favorite with Hollywood stars, including such disparate personalities over the years as Tallulah Bankhead, John

Barrymore, Clara Bow, Marlene Dietrich, W. C. Fields, Errol Flynn, Greta Garbo, the Marx Brothers, Pola Negri, and Gloria Swanson. Humphrey Bogart and Lauren Bacall honeymooned here. The hotel also attracted many top writers, who had come to Hollywood to work at the studios, including Robert Benchley, F. Scott Fitzgerald, Sheila Graham, and John O'Hara.

What was the reason for the extraordinary appeal of the Garden of Allah? It couldn't have been the hotel's cramped ill-furnished accommodations or less-than-palatable food. Probably the Garden of Allah's mystique came from its self-indulgent, anything-goes spirit. Orson Welles secretly met stripper Lili St. Cyr in his Garden of Allah room, which was located just below Nazimova's apartment in the main building. And actress Mary Astor and playwright George S. Kaufman used one of the hotel bungalows for their affair, which became front-page gossip across the nation when Mary's cuckolded husband leaked incriminating excerpts from her no-holds-barred diary at the time of their divorce trial. "Once George lays down his glasses, he is *quite* a different man" read one of Mary Astor's reported entries. "His powers of recuperation are amazing, and we made love all night long. . . . It all worked perfectly, and we shared our fourth climax at dawn."

The Sunset Strip's heyday did not last much past World War II. In 1950, the Garden of Allah was demolished because of its obsolescence and increasingly unsavory reputation. By the late 1950s, most of the nightclubs had closed, because they could not afford the salaries that Las Vegas hotels were paying leading entertainers.

Nature abhors a vacuum, as does urban real estate. After the lavish prewar nightclubs had sat empty for several years, less expensive, more youth-oriented clubs and coffeehouses took over the buildings in the 1960s. Thanks to the county laws, proprietors could welcome minors, on condition that they did not order liquor.

The Sunset Strip was "hot" again, much to the dismay of nearby residents who were appalled to see thousands of pleasure-loving young people strolling up and down the sidewalks at all hours or creating monumental Friday- and Saturday-night

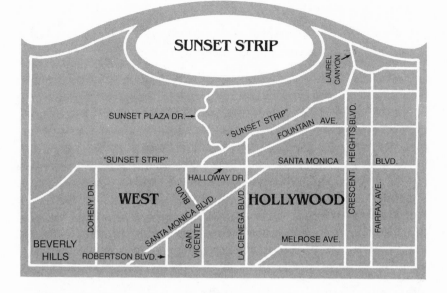

traffic jams as they cruised the street. In the late 1960s and 1970s, the situation grew even tenser as the Sunset Strip became a Hippie haven, thereby attracting more footloose men and women and driving long-established shops and businesses from the area.

Today, the 1.5-mile long Sunset Strip is one of the best-known parts of Los Angeles. But it has a serious identity crisis. The street, for one thing, can't decide what it is: a shopping area for the neighborhood, a business district, an entertainment spot, or a place for tourists to stay. As a result, the Sunset Strip is a confused jumble of shops, office buildings, restaurants, apartments, nightclubs, and hotels, of all different sizes and vintages.

To make the Sunset Strip's image even more confusing, the street has vastly different economic gradations, which coexist warily with each other. By virtue of its location between expensive hillside homes and generally desirable West Hollywood apartments, the Sunset Strip should have a more polished appearance, as it does near Sunset Plaza Drive or the few blocks just east of Beverly Hills. Yet, as a result of hard times in the 1960s and 1970s, much of the Sunset Strip's remaining blocks look slightly run down, an appearance made worse by all the coffeeshops, liquor stores, and often-raucous music clubs.

73

At present, the Sunset Strip exists in this uneasy state of limbo. Although some boosters predict that the street is on the upswing, by virtue of its location, the Sunset Strip could go either way in the future or remain virtually the same.

SUNSET STRIP TOUR

Despite its glamorous past and its well-known name today, the Sunset Strip is not well suited to traditional sightseeing. In other words, you will be disappointed if you walk down the street carefully studying one building after another. There isn't that much to *see*.

Instead you should *experience* the Sunset Strip in one of two ways. You can visit some of the unusual shops, fine restaurants, and popular music clubs along the street. Or, if this approach seems too time-consuming and expensive, simply drive down the Sunset Strip. Better yet, ask a friend to take the wheel so that you don't have to concentrate on driving. And be sure to visit the Sunset Strip at night. What you notice is the handful of spotlit landmark buildings like the Chateau Marmont, the brightly lit store signs and looming billboards which tout the latest singer or movie, and the moving lines of car headlights and tail lights snaking around the curves.

If enjoying the Sunset Strip this way sounds appealing, wait until a Friday or a Saturday night in good weather. The energy level is even higher than usual, because young people cruise up and down the street and fill the sidewalks as they stroll from one music club to another or wait for a show to begin.

LA TOQUE   *8171 Sunset Boulevard. West Hollywood. Monday–Friday, noon to 3:00 P.M. and 6:00 P.M. to 10:30 P.M.; Saturday, 6:30 P.M. to 10:30 P.M. Telephone: 656-7515. Expensive. All major credit cards. Valet parking.*

In most of the world, gifted young cooks face years of low-paid apprenticeships and then more years of working in another chef's kitchen before they have the opportunity of opening their own restaurant. But with restaurants, as in so many other things, Los Angeles has started a new trend: under-thirty-year-old chefs almost routinely start their own establishments, often very deluxe ones at that.

By any measure, Ken Frank is one of the most successful of these precocious chef/proprietaires. After wowing most of the critics and food-loving Angelenos at several restaurants in the late 1970s, the Pasadena-born Frank opened La Toque in a charming one-story stucco building, which most recently had housed La Ruche for one year and before that the short-lived, often-tumultuous La Guillotine.

In its present reincarnation, with its beamed ceilings, roughly textured stucco walls, and mock-Louis chairs whose wood frames resemble tree branches, the light and airy restaurant looks something like a mix between a French country inn and a Southern California patio-gone-elegant. Whatever its style, La Toque creates a pleasant atmosphere, and once guests take their tables they would never guess that traffic-filled Sunset Boulevard lies on the other side of the lace-curtained windows.

Ken Frank favors a French-inspired nouvelle cuisine, which is directly influenced by the Japanese traditions. La Toque's menu offers appetizers such as artichoke bottoms, bay scallops, and lobster in a delicate cream sauce; wild mushroom soup; warm slices of eel on red lettuce leaves with watercress, enoki-dake mushrooms, and sesame seeds; tiny Santa Barbara shrimp in a subtle mustard sauce; and pasta stuffed with lobster. The equally inventive entrées might include a scallop mousse in a crayfish sauce, slices of rabbit with basil on a bed of homemade noodles, fresh salmon poached in a rich Sauternes wine and adorned with rose petals, or roast tarragon-scented saddle of lamb served with precisely cut and slightly undercooked slices of carrot and zucchini.

Some diners find Frank's subtle flavors to be just a little boring and his almost-Japanese emphasis on presentation somewhat precious. But most guests love his inventive medley of flavors and textures and the it's-almost-too-beautiful-to-eat appearances of the various dishes. You may order your meal from the à la carte side of the menu or select the five-course prix-fixe "menu fantasie," which changes every day and includes an appetizer, a fish course, a meat course, a selection of well-chosen cheeses, and dessert and coffee.

For all its virtues, La Toque still has a way to go before it joins the select ranks of Los Angeles' consistently fine restaurants. Ken Frank can be erratic as well as brilliant in the kitchen. Some of the waiters can be unnecessarily huffy considering their serving skills. The menu is all in French, a needless translation chore for English-speaking-only guests who left their Berlitz *French for Travellers* phrase book at home.

CHATEAU MARMONT HOTEL   *8221 Sunset Boulevard. Telephone: 656-1010.*

Everyone in Los Angeles knows about the Chateau Marmont Hotel—it's the 1920s Normanesque castle rising above the gaudy billboards at the broad curve that marks mere Sunset Boulevard's transformation into the Sunset Strip just west of Crescent Heights Boulevard. It's the one-time favorite hotel of Clark Gable, Jean Harlow, and Carole Lombard, which now has become popular with visiting actors, artists, and writers. It was here in one of the garden bungalows that comedian John Belushi died of a drug overdose.

The Chateau Marmont's credentials as a show business institution are firmly established. But what is the hotel like simply as a place to stay? If you cringe at the thought of the typical big-city business hotel, and instead enjoy a spirit of individuality or the aura of old Hollywood, stay at the Chateau Marmont by all means. As a hotel, the building is one of a kind in Los Angeles, and it even is an official city landmark. And the Chateau Marmont's lobby is a step back in time with its beamed wood ceiling, large arched windows overlooking the front garden, and an Oriental rug and antique furniture, not to mention an out-of-tune piano that daring guests play occasionally.

But if you primarily are looking for comfort and chic appearances in a hotel, steer clear of the Chateau Marmont. The overall mood is "genteel shabby," with a slight imbalance of shabbiness over gentility, in things like weeds in some planting areas or downright dowdy rooms and clanging pipes. Services are meager, and the hotel lacks a restaurant or a bar.

Despite these genuine failings, the Chateau Marmont has a distinctive 1920s Los Angeles charm all its own, something that probably could not be duplicated elsewhere these days. When some of its newer and glossier rivals have faded past the point of no return, the Chateau Marmont probably will still be going its own eccentric way as the self-proclaimed "favorite of the famous."

� ■■■ **SOURCE** ■■■ *8301 Sunset Boulevard. West Hollywood. Monday–Friday, 11:00 A.M. to midnight; Saturday–Sunday, 9:00 A.M. to midnight. Telephone: 656-6388. Moderate. American Express, MasterCard, and VISA credit cards. Parking lot.*

A few years ago, the Source was quite a joy to discover— hearty soups, sandwiches, salads, and meat and fish entrées, all carefully prepared from the freshest possible organically raised ingredients. What's more, this casual and reasonably priced restaurant offered three totally different dining areas to choose from: an open patio behind a wall in front, a medium-size funkily comfortable dining room filled with wooden tables and chairs just inside the front door, and a separate and more intimate room with just three booths.

Recently, the Source seems to have lost something of its earlier magic. Maybe the kitchen doesn't care as much about meal preparation as it once did. Or perhaps newer, more sophisticated organic-style restaurants have come along, while the Source remains the same. Still, this restaurant remains a good value for snacks or a quick meal in the Sunset Strip area. But skip the outdoor patio unless you like shouting over the noise of passing cars and trucks.

Does the Source look familiar when you see it for the first

time? It should. In the movie *Annie Hall,* Diane Keaton tells Woody Allen to go back to New York in a scene filmed at the restaurant.

🏠 **SUNSET TOWERS**   *8358 Sunset Boulevard.*

When the conversation turns to historic architecture, most Angelenos think of the Spanish Colonial Revival style of the 1920s. But older Los Angeles is very much a Moderne city of the 1930s as well. Often called Art Deco, the Moderne style usually consists of an impressive monumentality, unbroken upward-reaching vertical lines, clean surfaces ornamented by zigzags, chevrons, sunbursts, even stylized animals or machinery, and sometimes a central tower which steps back from the primary vertical façade plane. On truly extravagant Moderne buildings, the façade might consist of terra-cotta tiles in a variety of colors.

The Sunset Towers apartments is one of Los Angeles' best known Moderne buildings, not just for its intrinsic architectural qualities but also because it is one of the few really outstanding Moderne structures in this part of Los Angeles. The finest Moderne buildings usually stand in downtown Los Angeles, along older sections of Wilshire Boulevard, or on Hollywood Boulevard, which were the primary locations for expensive commercial development during the 1930s. The Sunset Towers is even more noticeable, because it is one of the few older high-rise buildings on the Sunset Strip. Think of the views over Los Angeles from most apartments. And don't miss the stylized automobile grill decorations at the building's garage.

🎭 **COMEDY STORE**   *8433 Sunset Boulevard. Admission charge. Telephone: 656-6225.*

Formerly the site of Ciro's nightclub, the Comedy Store has been one of the most important showcases for Los Angeles comedians during the last decade. You can watch up-and-coming comics striving to reach the top as well as top stars who are trying out new routines before heading off to Las Vegas. Call the Comedy Store for up-to-the-minute details.

HELPFUL HINT: Street parking on the Sunset Strip is almost impossible on weekend evenings. And parking is illegal on many nights along the elegant residential streets north of the Strip. Fortunately, the Comedy Store has valet parking. Drop off your car in the hotel driveway next door.

SUNSET PLAZA · *8578–8623 Sunset Boulevard.*

Sunset Plaza is a cluster of fashionable one- and two-story neoclassical-style shops, which were built in the 1930s according to a master plan. The parking is located in the rear of the buildings, which permits the shop fronts to line the sidewalk, thereby clearly defining the space of the street and providing a pleasant place to stroll or to window-shop.

Compare Sunset Plaza's coherent sense of style and its avowedly urban spirit to almost any other shopping street in Los Angeles, and you will see how much today's developers have to learn about design, even though this attractive and practical example of the shopping strip has existed for fifty years.

SPAGO *8795 Sunset Boulevard. West Hollywood. Open seven days, 6:00 P.M. to 11:30 P.M. Telephone: 652-4025. Expensive. All major credit cards. Valet parking.*

The moment that Spago opened during 1982, it immediately became Los Angeles' "in" restaurant. One evening, no fewer than twenty-seven Rolls-Royces sat in the parking lot. Before guests even reached the front doors, they first passed several photographers who were waiting for celebrities to appear. And once guests entered the large pastel-shaded dining room, they were dazzled by the bright lights of Los Angeles stretching for miles outside the picture windows, not to mention all the beauti-ful—or at least hard to miss—show biz folk eating their dinners.

Can the food at a restaurant this fashionable be any good? Yes. In fact, it's excellent, thanks to Wolfgang Puck, former chef at Ma Maison for six years, who wanted a restaurant of his own.

Spago's specialty is pizza, which is baked in a brick oven at one side of the dining room. But you probably have never eaten pizza quite like this, or have ever seen pizza served on a Villeroy & Boch plate. Try the duck sausage pizza, or one topped with tiny Santa Barbara shrimp, or another covered by fresh to-matoes, onions, and goat cheese.

Share one of the small pizzas as an appetizer, then move onto the even more exquisite nouvelle French-inspired grown-up dishes, like fresh marinated tuna with avocado, green salads with baked goat cheese, angel-hair pasta topped with one half a perfectly roast and sliced squab, or a whole baked red snapper in an onion and butter sauce.

Spago has an outdoor terrace, but take a table in the sparsely furnished high-tech-inspired dining room, even though it is un-comfortably noisy at times. Where else can you eat fabulous food, at less-than-horrifying prices, and overhear the conversa-tions of your favorite soap opera star who is sitting at the next table?

$ **TOWER RECORDS** *8801 Sunset Boulevard. Telephone: 657-7300.*

This store is a Los Angeles institution, not only for its extraor-dinary selection of records and tapes, but also for the ecletic-looking shoppers. Late Friday and Saturday night are the best time for people-watching. The Annex across the street at 8844 Sunset Boulevard features an amazing collection of classical recordings.

The Sunset Strip

🎭 **ROXY** *9009 Sunset Boulevard. Telephone: 276-2222.*

The Roxy is the top music club in Los Angeles. The music industry often showcases promising talents here or books an established star who wants to promote a new album. The sound system is one of the best in town. And the Art Deco-style interior is glamorous-looking. Call the Roxy for latest information about acts and prices. Valet parking is available.

🎭 **GAZZARRI'S** *9039 Sunset Boulevard. Telephone: 273-6606.*

Now in its twentieth year, Gazzari's is the oldest music club on the Sunset Strip. What is their secret of longevity in this notoriously fickle business? Good music and plenty of it, whether you want to listen or head for one of the two dance floors. Tuesday, Wednesday, and Thursday are showcase nights. Local bands perform on Friday and Saturday nights. Show-business-history buffs take note: Barbi Benton got her start as Miss Gazzarri of 1968. You don't know who Barbi Benton is?

✗ **SCANDIA** *9040 Sunset Boulevard. West Hollywood. Tuesday–Saturday, 11:30 A.M. to 3:00 P.M. and 6:00 P.M. to midnight; Sunday, 5:00 P.M. to 11:30 P.M.; Sunday brunch, 11:00 A.M. to 3:00 P.M. Telephone: 278–3555. Expensive to very expensive. All major credit cards. Valet parking.*

By any measure Scandia is one of Los Angeles' restaurant landmarks, along with Chasen's, Musso & Frank's, and Ma Maison, to name several. On November 7, 1946, the gifted yet hot-tempered Ken Hansen opened the first Scandia on the Sunset Strip at the present site of La Maganette. By the time Hansen moved across the street to Scandia's current chalet-style building on February 4, 1958, many food critics regularly hailed his restaurant as the finest in all Los Angeles.

No one could seriously make that claim about Scandia today. It's not that the cuisine has slipped that much under the ownership of publishing baron Robert Petersen. Rather the reason is that the gastronomic competition has gotten much fiercer in Los Angeles, and Scandia has stood still. Think of the exquisite meals at L'Ermitage, Rex, or Michael's, and you'll see how much the local restaurant scene has changed.

Despite its somewhat dated mood and look, Scandia remains as popular as ever, and it has become something of a club for business people and couples who have been coming here for decades. And each one of these regulars has a favorite place to sit, whether it is the spacious, high-ceilinged main dining room, which has colorful blue-leather booths and assorted Scandinavian touches like shields and plates on the paneled walls; the airy Belle Terrasse with its profusion of fresh flowers and trellises; the masculine Skaal Room with its bar; or the small, oak-paneled Danish Room where copper pans decorate the walls. In all, Scandia can accommodate 250 guests at once.

What do all these people find in the way of food? The vast part Scandinavian/part Continental menu offers such superb appetizers as smoked salmon, gravlaxs, shrimp in dill, matjes herring, or Hamlet's dagger, which is lobster tails served on a dagger and flamed in aquavit. The smoked eel, which arrives from Denmark on S.A.S. like many of the fish appetizers, is sensational with its rich, almost-meaty texture and delicately smoked flavor.

Moving onto the entrées, Scandia offers several dozen more-or-less standard Continental-style dishes, like saddle of lamb, veal scaloppini sole meunière, or fresh game in season. The Scandinavian entrées are more interesting, such as biff Lindstrom (chopped beef with beets, capers, and onions) or the Kalldolmar (cabbage filled with seasoned beef and pork). The meals end on a down note with mediocre coffee and desserts that look much better than they actually taste.

Scandia serves a reasonably priced supper menu after 10

P.M. Its wine list is a marvel, with hundreds of California wines, plus older French Bordeaux and Burgundies at fair prices.

For all its commendable qualities,, Scandia can be a disappointment due to the service. Occasionally the waiters are so disorganized that they ask for your order after someone else has just taken it. Or they don't know what vegetables are still available in the kitchen and take five minutes to find out. But some of the waiters' attitudes are even more annoying. For a few regulars, the staff can be smoothly charming, but for everyone else, their mood ranges from perfunctorily polite to downright condescending, even to the point of bad-mouthing guests behind their backs.

✖️ COCK 'N BULL   *9170 Sunset Boulevard. West Hollywood. Monday–Friday, 11:30 A.M. to 11:00 P.M.; Saturday, 2:00 P.M. to 11:00 P.M. Buffet service available Monday–Friday, 11:30 A.M. to 2:30 P.M. and 6:00 P.M. to 11:00 P.M.; Saturday, 5:00 P.M. to 11:00 P.M.. On Sundays, the restaurant serves a buffet-style brunch from 10:00 A.M. to 2:30 P.M. Telephone : 276-7814. Open all holidays. Moderate. American Express, Diners' Club, MasterCard, and VISA credit cards.*

Located on the Sunset Strip just east of Beverly Hills, the Cock 'N Bull has been open for over forty years, and considering its good value and pleasant ambience, this restaurant should be around for another forty years. Once you drop off your car with the parking attendants and step through the front door, the ever-throbbing Sunset Strip, indeed all of Los Angeles, seems far away.

The Cock 'N Bull looks very, very British with its dimly lit dining rooms, plaid carpeting, and dark-paneled walls that are decorated with pewter plates, swords, tartans, and other Anglo-Saxon paraphernalia. The well-prepared food is equally British. You can order from the menu. Or you can try the fixed-price all-you-can-eat buffet. If you select the buffet, and most patrons do, waitresses will bring Welsh rarebit, soup, or fruit cup to your table, followed by a salad. Then you head for the buffet, which offers delicious roast beef and Yorkshire pudding, steak and kidney pie, curries, duck, ham, and fresh sliced turkey, plus an assortment of potatoes and vegetables. By the time the wait-resses bring your coffee and desserts, someone at your table invariably has remarked that the food at the Cock 'N Bull is better than anything they ate during their recent trip to Great Britain.

Whatever the pros and cons of British cooking, that nation's hearty breakfasts are world-famous, and the Cock 'N Bull con-tinues this noble tradition with its Sunday brunch, which con-sists of eggs, sausage, kippers, finnan haddie, to name a few offerings.

P.S. If you're feeling expansive and more than a little British by the end of your meal at the Cock 'N Bull, you can stroll over to the Jaguar® showroom, which is located several doors away at 9176 Sunset Boulevard.

8
West Hollywood

BACKGROUND

Approximately bounded by Fairfax Avenue on the east, the Sunset Strip on the north, Third Street on the south, and the Beverly Hills city limits on the west, West Hollywood is a physical extension of Hollywood, as the name implies, but any real resemblance between the two communities largely ends there.

Outside of the busy commercial thoroughfares like Santa Monica Boulevard and Melrose Avenue, West Hollywood's housing is a similar mixture of bungalows, two- and four-unit apartments, and large modern apartments and condominiums, but these buildings almost invariably are better maintained than those in Hollywood. Unlike the Hollywood streets several miles to the east, West Hollywood has a largely Anglo population, and many of its residents are gay men who frequent some of the bars, shops, and restaurants along Santa Monica Boulevard between Fairfax Avenue and Robertson Boulevard.

85

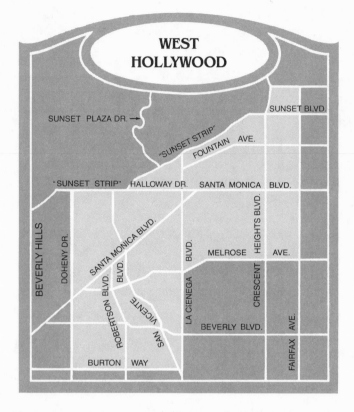

WEST
HOLLYWOOD

SUNSET BLVD.

SUNSET PLAZA DR. →

"SUNSET STRIP"

FOUNTAIN AVE.

"SUNSET STRIP" HALLOWAY DR. SANTA MONICA BLVD.

BEVERLY HILLS

DOHENY DR.

SANTA MONICA BLVD.

ROBERTSON BLVD.

BLVD.

SAN VICENTE

LA CIENEGA BLVD.

MELROSE AVE.

CRESCENT HEIGHTS BLVD.

BEVERLY BLVD.

FAIRFAX AVE.

BURTON WAY

While most of West Hollywood is generally considered a good place to live, it is an even chicer place for the Hollywood Hills or Beverly Hills well-to-do to go shopping, eat at restaurants, or buy home furnishings. Robertson Boulevard's "Decorators' Row," L'Ermitage, Melrose Place, L'Orangerie, the Pacific Design Center, Chasen's—you'll find all these high-level consumer landmarks in West Hollywood, and more.

But West Hollywood is becoming a victim of its own success as well. The hulking Beverly Center is one of the worst recent buildings in Los Angeles, both as a single work of architecture and for the impact of its traffic on the surrounding neighborhood. Skip this urban atrocity unless you are a hopeless shopping center addict. And so many apartments and condominiums are replacing the 1920s and 1930s bungalows and flats on West Hollywood's side streets that the developers may soon destroy much of the urban charm that their buildings are trying to take advantage of.

[$] **"DECORATORS' ROW"**   *Robertson Boulevard, from Burton Way to Santa Monica Boulevard.*

Ten years ago, this one-mile stretch of Robertson Boulevard was solidly entrenched as the center of Los Angeles' thriving interior-design trade. Furniture, antiques, fabrics, and accessories showrooms and manufacturers' "reps" lined both sides of the street, especially between Melrose Avenue and Beverly Boulevard, and they sold only to architects, designers, and decorators.

Today, Robertson Boulevard is suffering an identity crisis. In the late 1970s, many of the "to the trade only" showrooms, including Kneedler-Fauchère, Brunschwig et Fils, and Stark Carpets, moved to the blue glass-walled Pacific Design Center at San Vicente Boulevard and Melrose Avenue, a block east of Robertson.

Although some showrooms, like Scalamandre, F. Schumacher, and Greeff, still remain on Robertson Boulevard, the street is more and more becoming the location for fashionable *retail* furniture and antique stores, as well as chic art galleries, clothing boutiques, and restaurants. If going from shop to shop doesn't really appeal to you, try half an hour of window-shopping on Robertson between Beverly Boulevard and Melrose Avenue in the early evening. The brightly lit window displays are quite pleasing, even if you're not a "shop-aholic."

HELPFUL HINT: Every showroom or shop on Robertson Boulevard has its own policy about serving the general public. Of course, the retail establishments will welcome you—and your checkbook—with open arms, while quietly offering discounts to members of the trade. Don't be intimidated by the snooty-acting and -looking salesclerks in some stores. If you can afford to shop there, you earn much more money than they do.

Some Robertson Boulevard showrooms and shops, which

post the "to the trade only" signs, will let you look around, and occasionally they may permit you to buy something, again at a higher price than someone in the business. And some really "high-heeled" showrooms—that means "high end"—won't even let you past the front door unless you are accompanied by your architect or decorator. Avoid embarrassment. When you walk into a showroom, ask the person at the front desk about their policy regarding the public.

Start at Burton Way, the southern end of the traditional "Decorators' Row" and head north. NOTE: For Robertson Boulevard addresses, Beverly Boulevard marks the dividing line between "North" and "South." The farther south of Beverly, the higher the South Robertson address will be. Conversely, as you head north of Beverly, the North Robertson addresses get higher.

Burton S. Klein, *315 South Robertson. Accessories.*

Michel Richard Restaurant, *310 South Robertson. Monday–Saturday, 9:00 A.M. to 7:00 P.M. Telephone: 275–5707. Moderate. MasterCard and VISA credit cards.*

On the back of his menu, Michel Richard quotes Antonin Carême, the early nineteenth-century founder of haute cuisine, as declaring: "The fine arts are six in number: painting, sculpture, poetry, music, architecture, and pastry." Therefore, it should be no surprise to learn that Richard was a pastry chef before he became a caterer in Los Angeles and opened his casual and highly regarded café in the middle of "Decorators' Row."

In keeping with its early evening closing time, Michel Richard mostly offers light meals, which are perfect for a lingering late breakfast, a festive lunch, or a late afternoon snack. The menu lists country pâtés, several large salads—French chicken is by far the best—various quiches, and enormous fluffy omelettes—mushroom, ham and gruyère cheese, chives and parsley, and the filling *paysanne* (bacon, onion, and potatoes). Every day Michel Richard also prepares about ten equally delicious specials, like sautéed lamb with rosemary, salmon tournedos with bell pepper, hazelnut trout, and endive salad with sweetbreads.

Of course, the restaurant's pièce de résistance is Michel Richard's pastry, which is tantalizingly displayed on the right as you walk in. When it's time for dessert, get up from your chair and make your selection from the case. Sugar, butter, and white flour rarely taste this good. The coffee, however, makes a mediocre end to an otherwise enjoyable meal.

[$] **Soleil,** *120 South Robertson. Contemporary furniture and accessories.*

[$] **Jay Clark,** *110 South Robertson. Traditional fabrics and reproductions. Antique furniture.*

[$] **Gallery West,** *107 South Robertson. Art gallery.*

[$] **Designer's Contemporary Art,** *103 South Robertson. Art gallery.*

[$] **Snyder-Diamond,** *100 South Robertson. "High end" items like solid-brass door hardware, the latest in stovetops, and deluxe bathroom accessories. Open to the public.*

[$] **L. A. Desserts,** *113 North Robertson. Just what the name says. Fabulous.*

✗ **The Ivy,** *113 North Robertson. Telephone: 273-5537.*

Owned by L. A. Desserts, the Ivy is a great spot for a late breakfast or light lunch, particularly if you get a table on the outdoor terrace. In 1983, the restaurant extended its hours and started serving dinners that emphasize fresh fish, salads, California vegetables, and of course the incredible desserts.

[$] **F. Schumacher,** *116 North Robertson. Fabrics.*

[$] **Paul Associates,** *147 North Robertson. Steel and lucite furniture.*

[$] **Fortress, Inc.,** *8801 Beverly Boulevard. "High end" office furniture.*

✗ **Sundance Café,** *350 North Robertson. Telephone: 659-1485.*

Pleasant WASP-style Mexican food, plus hamburgers, sandwiches, and salads.

[$] **Ralph B. Reilly,** *449 North Robertson. Antiques.*

✗ **Patio Restaurant,** *450 North Robertson. Telephone: 659-8381.*

As the name implies, this pleasant restaurant offers outdoor dining—with a roof overhead, however—in warm weather. For winter and cool summer evenings they roll down the clear plastic "walls" and turn on the heaters. The Patio serves everything from omelettes to chicken and steak, including good salads and hamburgers.

[$] **Raymond & Keith,** *451 North Robertson. Country antiques.*

[$] **Tiberio,** *458 Robertson. Antiques, particularly Art Deco-style.*

[✗] **Ed's Coffee Shop,** *460 North Robertson.*

Almost hidden behind its faded pink and white plastic awning, Ed's is a Robertson Boulevard institution. Come here in the morning and watch the chicly attired decorators eat truck-stop-style food in the classic coffeeshop setting. Start a good rumor here in the morning, and the whole trade will know it by late afternoon.

[$] **Designer's Floor Coverings,** *471 North Robertson. The name says it all.*

[$] **David & Dash,** *474 North Robertson. Fabrics.*

[$] **The Linen Trees,** *501 North Robertson. Everything for the bedroom and bath. Open to the public.*

[$] **Appalachian Arts,** *511 North Robertson. Arts and crafts. Open to the public.*

[$] **Kaleidoscope,** *517 North Robertson. Gifts and accessories. Open to the public.*

Melrose Avenue intersects Robertson Boulevard here. See the 8700 block entries under the Melrose Avenue Tour for the show-rooms near Robertson Boulevard.

[🏠] *Architectural Delights.* **Bowser Boutique,** *608 North Robertson.*

Skip the building. Check out the larger-than-life statue of "bowser" sitting in front. What do the local decorators think of his bright orange-and-black color scheme? Also, see the "log cabin" at 621 North Robertson and the "Olde English" building with half-timbered and properly faded red-brick walls at nearby 646 North Robertson.

[$] **Dennis & Leen,** *612 North Robertson. Antiques.*

This showroom is so exclusive that they pull down the shades in the front windows at night, lest the pedestrian hoi polloi admire the treasures within.

[✗] **Rose Tattoo Restaurant,** *665 North Robertson. Monday–Friday, noon to 3:00 P.M. and 6:30 P.M. to 11:00 P.M., Saturday, 6:30 P.M. to 11:00 P.M., Sunday, noon to 3:00 P.M. for brunch and 6:30 P.M. to 11:00 P.M. for dinner. Valet parking. Telephone: 854-4455. Expensive. All major cards.*

90

Upon arriving at the Rose Tattoo, you can sense that this is a great place for lunch or dinner. The maître d' greets you like an old friend, even if you haven't been to the restaurant in months. And the main dining room, just inside the front door, has an elegant yet comfortable look with its part-mirrored, part-upholstered walls, gray twill-covered chairs and banquettes, and soft, flattering lighting. Even the graphics hanging on the walls are good, and all depict a rose theme. Only the decorative purists among the largely male clientele will make a big deal about the clumsy handling of the beams and mirrors on the main dining room ceiling.

Is the Rose Tattoo all show and no substance like more than a few Hollywood restaurants? Not in the least. The meals rival those at some of Los Angeles better known "gourmet restaurants," but the prices are fairly reasonable, if you order the prix fixe dinner, which almost everyone does.

Start with an appetizer like pasta salad niçoise, chicken croquettes, Caesar salad, or the astonishing "crûdités Rose Tattoo," which is a large wicker basket filled with all kinds of thinly sliced and carefully arranged raw vegetables, served with several sauces for dipping. Next comes the soup of the day and, after that, an entrée like shrimp Pernod and rice, veal sautéed with Roquefort sauce, linguini with Norwegian smoked salmon, or whitefish sautéed with golden caviar. Or you may want either the day's duck or chicken preparation.

If a meal at the Rose Tattoo has a flaw, it is trying to find room on the two-person tables for the salt and pepper shakers, the vase which holds a single rose, the silverware, the bread basket, and the complimentary bowl of terrific duck rillette. But this small problem is quickly forgotten as you enjoy the food and the friendly yet entirely professional service. When the busboys clear away the entrée plates before dessert, for example, they also remove the salt and pepper shakers. Where else but the Rose Tattoo are you going to find this quality of food and service in a restaurant where you can also wear casual clothes and still not feel out of place?

$\boxed{\$}$ **International Terra Cotta,** *690 North Robertson.*

Pots like you didn't know existed, and usually don't outside of this establishment.

🏠 **FOUNTAIN AVENUE TOUR** *Hayworth Avenue to La Cienega Boulevard.*

START: *Fountain and Hayworth avenues.*

TIME: *One hour.*

For many Angelenos and visitors, this three-quarter-mile stretch of Fountain Avenue is just a quick east-to-west thoroughfare that avoids most of the congestion and stoplights of Sunset Boulevard to the north or Santa Monica Boulevard to the south. But if these drivers slowed down and studied Fountain Avenue, as well as some of the adjacent side streets, they would see that this part of West Hollywood has some of the handsomest and most livable apartment buildings in all Los Angeles.

Following an east-to-west route along Fountain Avenue, start at Hayworth Avenue, which is two blocks east of Crescent Heights Boulevard. Turn right onto Hayworth Avenue and drive north until you reach number 1433, where in 1940 F. Scott Fitzgerald died of a heart attack in British gossip columnist Sheila Graham's apartment.

Turn around and return to Fountain Avenue. Go one block, then turn right on Laurel Avenue. Stop at 1355 North Laurel, which is halfway up the block on your left. You won't see the number from the street, but you will spot the half-Spanish, half-Italian-style 1928 apartment building at once, because it is more impressive-looking than anything else on the block.

Park your car and take a closer look. From the street, you see a landscaped walkway in the middle of the **VILLA D'ESTE** and a garage building on either side. But these garages have not been tacked onto the front of this apartment complex as an afterthought. Instead, they are an integral part of the design with their arched doors, which are separated by pilasters, mellow brick walls, and attractively faded red-tile roofs, not to mention the patterned terra cotta driveways.

Follow the walkway between the garages, past the rectangular tile-edged pond with a lion's head that spouts water, and proceed through the tall, dimly lit archway into the Villa d'Este's central courtyard. How many modern apartment buildings have a public space this charming or peaceful? In the center, you find a splashing fountain that adds sound and a feeling of coolness to the courtyard, which is landscaped with lemon, olive, and banana trees. Around the sides, each apartment has its own entrance and a small walled garden. Do not disturb the occupants.

Just up the block, notice 1401 North Laurel, a gray Normandyesque apartment building where F. Scott Fitzgerald lived in apartment six while writing his final novel, *The Last Tycoon,* which was unfinished at the time of his death.

Return to your car, turn around, and head south down Laurel Avenue, until you reach Fountain Avenue, where you turn right and head west. At the southwest corner of Fountain Avenue and Crescent Heights Boulevard, you see the **LA FONTAINE APART-MENTS** (get it?), which is a local landmark because of its balustraded terrace above street level, soft red-brick French château-esque façade, and picturesquely steep roof.

One block past Crescent Heights, turn right on Havenhurst Drive, and park your car. At 1400–1414 North Havenhurst, admire the attractively massed Spanish-style façade of the **RONDA APARTMENTS,** which were completed in 1927 by Arthur and Mira Zwebell, an extraordinary Middle Western couple who moved to Los Angeles in 1921, then designed *and* built some of Hollywood and West Hollywood's finest courtyard-style apartment buildings until the time of the Depression.

Because the Ronda has solid wood doors rather than arches opening into the interior, you probably won't be able to see that the building's twenty apartments are arranged along two landscaped walkways instead of around one central courtyard. The apartments at the Ronda are unusually individualistic. All have their own entrances. Some duplex units boast two-story living rooms with a stairway and balcony leading to the second-floor bedrooms. A few apartments are vine-covered Spanish-style cottages.

Farther up the block, the red brick **COLONIAL HOUSE** at 1416 North Havenhurst was the home of William Powell and Carole Lombard after their 1931 marriage. Now Bette Davis lives here.

A little farther beyond, 1471–1475 North Havenhurst is **THE ANDALUSIA,** another courtyard-style apartment building, completed by the Zwebells in 1926. Between the brick- and tile-roofed garages on the street, an open gate leads into the terra-cotta-tiled motor court, which has more arched garage doors on the left and right. Straight ahead, an archway passes through the building into the heavily planted central courtyard, which has a tile-decorated fountain in the middle and an arched working fire-place in one wall. Most of the Andalusia's nine apartments have two-story living rooms, including the unit where the Zwebells lived. The Andalusia has always been a popular address with ac-tors and actresses, and over the years some of the better-known show business residents have included Clara Bow, Jean Hagen, John Payne, Cesar Romero, and Teresa Wright.

NOSTALGIA LOVERS TAKE NOTE: The **GARDEN OF ALLAH** once stood farther up the hill at the southeast corner of Sunset Boule-vard and Havenhurst Drive. For more information about the Gar-den of Allah, see page 71.

Turn around and return to Fountain Avenue on foot, and go right. Immediately ahead on your right, notice the **PATIO DEL MORO** at 8225–8237 Fountain, a Zwebell courtyard building, embellished with Moorish motifs, such as horseshoe-shaped arches and latticed windows.

At the next corner, which is Harper Drive, turn right. Don't miss the **VILLA PRIMAVERA** at the northeast corner of Fountain and Harper. Set far back from the street beneath trees, the Villa Primavera was the first of the Zwebells' outstanding courtyard-style buildings, and when the mostly one-story Spanish-style structure was completed in 1923, only one other building stood in the immediate vicinity.

Walk several hundred feet up Harper Avenue until you reach De Longpre Avenue, passing several other handsome 1920s and 1930s apartment buildings along the way. Take a look down one-block-long **DE LONGPRE.**

None of the apartment buildings, which date from the 1930s to the 1960s, are particularly distinguished in its own right. But the street has an overall pleasant appearance, thanks to the uni-form rows of palm trees on either side and all the buildings' sim-ilar colors and two- to three-story scale.

Return to your car. You may end your Fountain Avenue tour here. Or you can drive several more blocks down Fountain to La

Cienega Boulevard, viewing a few additional prewar Spanish or French château-style apartment complexes along the way. None of these buildings, however, equals those that you have already seen.

P.S. By now, you may wonder why anyone so architecturally sensitive as the Zwebells would have built several of their deluxe courtyard-style apartment buildings along a noisy traffic-filled street like Fountain Avenue. Of course, the street wasn't this busy in the 1920s and 1930s. Furthermore, until it was drastically widened fifteen years ago in order to accommodate an additional lane of traffic in each direction, Fountain Avenue was lined with palm trees and the buildings on both sides had front gardens along the sidewalks.

TAIL-O-THE-PUP *311 North La Cienega Boulevard, northwest corner of Beverly Boulevard.*

Even vegetarian Los Angelenos who haven't eaten meat for years know about Tail-O-The-Pup, the hot dog stand that looks like a giant hot dog in a bun. Located across the street from the looming Beverly Center, Tail-O-The-Pup is probably Los Angeles' best-known example of 1920s and 1930s "symbolic architecture," which is so named because the buildings actually signify their function through their forms, such as the orange juice stand that looks like a 10-foot-high orange or the fast-food tamale restaurant shaped like a giant tamale.

In the rapidly growing Los Angeles of the 1920s and 1930s, symbolic architecture served an important function. All these larger-than-life hot dogs, oranges, and tamales were familiar, reassuring sights for the city's many newcomers, and these buildings became overnight landmarks in a city that was too new to have any of the traditional kind. Besides, symbolic architecture was fun to look at—and Los Angelenos didn't have to read store signs to reach their destinations. If they wanted to eat at the Chili Bowl Restaurant, they weren't going to end up at the Coffee Pot Coffee Shop instead.

$ **MELROSE PLACE**

Starting where Melrose Avenue turns southward just beyond Orlando Avenue and stretching a mere two and a half short blocks before ending at La Cienega Boulevard, Melrose Place is quiet, tree-lined, architecturally cohesive, and pretty, something that few West Hollywood streets can claim. Melrose Place also is West Hollywood's choicest commercial location, and it is mainly given over to furniture, antiques, fabrics, and accessories show-rooms and shops, much like Robertson Boulevard, only more exclusive.

Many Melrose Avenue establishments sell to the trade only, or they maintain different prices for the public and the profes-sionals. If you see something that you like, don't reach for your checkbook too fast. If the ever-so-elegant salesclerk says that the price is "37," he usually means $37,000, not $3,700. Should you suffer a heart attack from the prices, rest assured that Cedars-Sinai Hospital is just a few blocks away.

Beginning at La Cienega Boulevard and moving eastward, the highlights of Melrose Place are

$ **Quatrain,** *700 North La Cienega Boulevard, corner of Melrose Place. Antiques.*

$ **Charles Pollock,** *8478 Melrose Place. Antiques and repro-duction antique furniture.*

✕ **Le Restaurant,** *8475 Melrose Place.*

As you would expect from this tony location, Le Restaurant is incredibly beautiful, always dressy, and a favorite with celebri-ties and successful decorators. But the food, while very good, does not equal the ambience. But how many meals could?

$ **John Good,** *8469 Melrose Place. Antiques and accessories.*

$ **Paul Ferrante,** *8464 Melrose Place. Fascinating, often av-ant-garde furniture, accessories, and lighting.*

$ **Barbara Lockhart,** *8445 Melrose Place. Accessories.*

$ **Richard Lindley,** *8441 Melrose Place. Mostly lamps.*

$ **Bac St. Antiques Cie,** *8428 Melrose Place. Antiques.*

✕ **Teddy's Liquor Mart & Deli,** *8409 Melrose Place.*

Teddy's isn't much to look at, but that doesn't stop the local decorators from stopping by for the terrific pork roast sand-wiches.

96

L'ERMITAGE   *730 North La Cienega Boulevard, just north of Melrose Avenue. West Hollywood. Monday–Saturday, dinner until 10:30 P.M. Telephone: 652-5840. Very expensive. All major credit cards. Valet parking.*

In French, the word *l'ermitage* means "retreat" or "hideaway, " and in 1975 this is exactly the kind of elegant restaurant that Jean Bertranou created admist the chic galleries and antique stores along bustling La Cienega Boulevard. To the delight of Los Angeles gourmets, Bertranou also was an extraordinarily gifted and innovative chef, and L'Ermitage was often hailed as one of the finest French restaurants in Los Angeles.

After Bertranou's untimely death in 1980, his widow Lilliane and nephew Patrick inherited the restaurant, and assistant chef Michel Blanchet took over the kitchen. L'Ermitage's devotees held their breath. Would the outgoing, yet unassuming, then-thirty-one-year-old Blanchet be able to maintain Bertranou's rigorous standards? If he succeeded, would Blanchet merely duplicate the late master's cuisine or would he lead L'Ermitage onto new glories of his own making?

Four years later, the gastronomic verdict is in. Blanchet has preserved some of Bertranou's dishes, but he has also introduced his own creativity into the kitchen, thereby maintaining L'Ermitage's considerable magic. Order the artichoke salad with duck confit and truffles, the chilled cream of sea urchin soup seasoned with a hint of ginger, the creamy duck-liver mousse, the roast squab with wild mushrooms, the filet of baby lamb in a fresh tarragon and red wine sauce, or the flavorful ragout of lobster, scallops, and shrimp.

The quality of Blanchet's cuisine is challenged only by its aesthetics. The deceptively simple-sounding "lobster salad L'Ermitage" looks like a flower filling its large serving plate. The center is a mound of lightly sautéed and chopped Belgian endive. The surrounding petals are slices of lobster and tiny pieces of peeled tomato, which sit on a creamy, yet slightly tart green watercress sauce.

Despite its exalted cuisine, L'Ermitage's spirit is relaxed and unintimidating in keeping with its Southern California location, and once guests step through the windowed and curtained front doors, the restaurant looks like a casual French country inn, admittedly a luxurious one. Of the restaurant's four separate dining rooms, the front salon is the most comfortable with its handsome fireplace, brass chandelier, large tables covered with white linen tablecloths and tapestry-covered high-backed chairs, and restful forest-green carpeting. Antique prints and small paintings of fruit decorate the warm, natural suede walls. The tables are so spaciously arranged that guests enjoy a sense of privacy even when every seat in the room is taken.

MANDARIN COVE *Eighth floor of the Beverly Center, located at Beverly and La Cienega boulevards. Open seven days, 11:30 A.M. to 9:30 P.M. Telephone: 652-3742. Moderate. MasterCard and VISA credit cards. Three hours of free parking in the Beverly Center.*

When Mandarin Cove opened on the eighth floor "restaurant row" in the cavernous Beverly Center, Chinese food fanatics on Los Angeles' west side breathed a collective sigh of relief. No longer did they have to drive all the way to Chinatown for the freshest and tastiest possible Chinese seafood.

Of course, Mandarin Cove doesn't serve only seafood dishes. Inveterate meat eaters will find two dozen beef, chicken, and pork dishes to choose from. But make no mistake: Mandarin Cove's specialty is seafood, as if you need to be told this after you pass the tanks of live bass, catfish, and cod near the front door of the restaurant. At latest count, this restaurant offers well over one hundred seafood dishes, ranging from simpler entrées such as shrimp with snow peas and cod filet with black bean sauce to more unusual offerings such as garlic carp in hot pot, stir-fried eel with ginger, and scallops with ginger and green onions. Mandarin Cove's chefs also work wonders with delicate conch and the similar-tasting but far-rarer abalone. Try the conch with fresh greens or the whole abalone in oyster sauce.

For a Chinese restaurant below the luxury-price level, Mandarin Cove is quite attractive and comfortable, except for the angled mirrors on the walls, which allow you to spy on your neighbors' tables and, in turn, enable them to see yours. But this is a small nuisance in an otherwise pleasing restaurant, and the crowds that fill Mandarin Cove night after night seem to agree.

SCHINDLER HOUSE *833 North Kings Road. Telephone: 651-1510.*

In the 1920s and 1930s, Los Angeles architects and builders rummaged through history and geography books looking for styles with just the right picturesque, faraway, and hopefully salable look. Spanish. Olde English. Norman French. Arabian. Chinese. Even ancient Egyptian. Nothing seemed too outlandish.

Yet these decades also were a time of remarkable architectural creativity in Los Angeles, as men like Frank Lloyd Wright, Richard Neutra, and Irving Gill tried to develop more practical, more up-to-date styles, which sometimes became part of the emerging modern movement. Another leader of this architectural vanguard was Rudolph Schindler, who was born and trained in Vienna, worked in Chicago between 1915 and 1919, then came to Los Angeles in 1919 to supervise the construction of Aline Barnsdall's Hollyhock House for Frank Lloyd Wright.

When Wright closed his Los Angeles office in 1921, Schindler started his own practice, and for the next thirty years he designed mostly single-family houses. Something of an eccentric, Schindler reportedly gained inspiration for his highly individualistic style from the modern movement, Wright, and cubism, and his houses are best known for their complex forms and spatial arrangements, usually executed in inexpensive materials like concrete, stucco, and plywood.

One of Schindler's finest works was his own house and studio, which still stands behind a thick hedge on Kings Road in West Hollywood. Completed in 1922 using post-and-beam construction, the Schindler House has concrete slab floors and upright slab and glass walls, which are built around three sides of a patio in the rear of the lot.

But the house's floor plan is more interesting than its structure, because Schindler and his wife, Pauline, shared the dwelling with their friends, the Clyde Chaces. He was Schindler's engineer. The Schindlers' L-shaped wing consisted of an entrance hall, bathroom, and two studios on the first floor and a sleeping porch on the second. The Chaces' quarters were identical except that the L has been "flipped over," in order to enclose the three sides of the patio, which served as the outdoor living room. The Schindlers' and Chaces' L-shaped living quarters were joined in the common kitchen, where the women worked on alternate weeks so that they could "gain periods of respite from the incessant household rhythm," according to Schindler.

The Schindler House is being restored, and it is open to the public. For information, call 651-1510.

THE CONDOMINIUM-IZATION OF WEST HOLLYWOOD
As seen from Kings Road.

When you visit the Schindler House, take a look at the surrounding block of Kings Road, because it is a microcosm of the changes now sweeping much of West Hollywood, particularly the residential side streets between Santa Monica Boulevard and Melrose Avenue. Near the Schindler House, you can still find the single-family residences with deep front yards and gardens that once characterized this neighborhood. And you can hardly miss the three- and four-story apartment buildings which replaced many of the houses in the 1960s and 1970s. These boxy stucco apartments are ugly-looking and greedily cover every available square foot of land, right up to the lot line. But at least the rents were reasonable when the buildings were completed, something that usually isn't true about the apartments any more.

The latest development trend on Kings Road, indeed in much of West Hollywood, is several-story condominiums, which often are little more than "dressed-up" apartments whose mortgage payments, taxes, and maintenance charges cost the owners considerably more money than the same space in an apartment would run a renter, even taking tax deductions into account. Often planned during the frenzied late 1970s real estate boom, many of these condominiums were completed in the early 1980s bust, and consequently they sat empty, unless the developer became desperate enough to rent out the units.

9 Melrose Avenue

BACKGROUND

Melrose Avenue is one of Hollywood's major east-west boulevards, stretching six miles from Hoover Street near downtown Los Angeles to Doheny Drive at the edge of Beverly Hills. Because it runs along the southern edge of the Hollywood flats, Melrose Avenue never has enjoyed the cachet of streets near the Hollywood Hills to the north or the grandeur of Wilshire Boulevard to the south. Indeed, Melrose Avenue was a nondescript and utterly forgettable street, and except for the one-mile section nearest Beverly Hills, its one- and two-story shops contained combination grocery and liquor stores, used-furniture outlets, and laundromats.

Not any longer. While Hollywood Boulevard is a rundown travesty of its former glamorous self and Wilshire Boulevard's "Miracle Mile" doesn't look so miraculous any more, much of Melrose Avenue has come up fast in the last five years, way up.

Of course, Rodeo Drive has far more exclusive as well as predictable shops than Melrose Avenue. And the pedestrian crowds are much thicker and the rents far higher in Westwood. But Melrose Avenue now has a greater true vitality than either of these well-known parts of Los Angeles, thanks to entrepreneurs, shopkeepers, and artists who are often doing something genuinely creative and original, rather than following a proven corporate formula or opening yet another branch of a status-name store.

Probably more than any other single part of Los Angeles, Melrose Avenue reflects the latest developments in fashion, furniture, and restaurants. Some Angelenos already sense this. All week long, but particularly on Saturday afternoons, style-conscious young men and women promenade up and down the sidewalks and walk in and out of the shops and restaurants, which is a welcome change in automobile-dependent Los Angeles.

But different parts of Melrose Avenue attract different kinds of people, because the street is far too long to become a cohesive unit, as say several-block-long Sunset Plaza or Rodeo Drive. Between Doheny Drive and Fairfax Avenue, and especially in the westernmost mile between Doheny Drive and La Cienega Boulevard, Melrose Avenue presents its choicest façade: interior decorators' showrooms, smart clothing boutiques, expensive antiques stores, and fashionable restaurants.

At present, the hottest and "youngest"—and most rapidly improving—parts of Melrose Avenue is the one-mile stretch which begins several blocks east of Fairfax Avenue and ends at Highland Avenue. Reflecting a gentrification cycle which is occurring in most American cities, many of the low-rent neighborhood shops are closing, and trendy used-clothing stores, book and record shops, theaters, and fine restaurants are taking their places.

East of Highland Avenue, the still largely commercial Melrose Avenue ranges from so-so to downright grim, depending on which neighborhood it is passing through. Nonetheless, chic shops are now moving into this area, propelled by higher rents west of Highland Avenue.

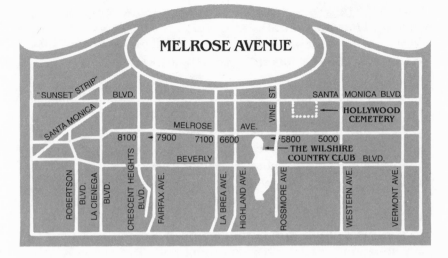

These rising rents could be a threat to Melrose Avenue's current anything-is-possible spirit as well as its long-range stability. If landlords get too greedy, the highly original shops and restaurants which give Melrose Avenue its special mood will be priced out of the area, and the high-volume, more commonplace operations will take their places, often only to open and close in quick succession as now happens on Rodeo Drive.

A more immediate threat to Melrose Avenue's rosy prospects is the highway department's plan to widen the street by one extra lane on either side. This is madness. Study the recently broadened blocks of Melrose Avenue east of La Cienega Boulevard. At six lanes width, the street becomes a visual and nearly functional barrier between the shops on either side. And the once-pleasant sidewalks are now so narrow that two people cannot walk together without one of them being impaled on the parking meters.

Whether or not local shopowners and residents can show the highway department the folly of this plan remains to be seen. But one thing is certain: For now, Melrose Avenue is the freshest, most exciting place to be in Hollywood, for that matter, probably in all Los Angeles. Enjoy it.

103

🍴 **CAFE FIGARO** *9010 Melrose Avenue. West Hollywood. Monday–Thursday, 11:30 A.M. to 12:30 A.M.; Friday–Saturday, 11:30 A.M. to 2:30 A.M.; Sunday, 4:00 P.M. to 12:30 A.M. Telephone: 274-7664. Moderate. MasterCard and VISA credit cards.*

At first impression, Café Figaro seems like quite a find. The omelettes, hamburgers, sandwiches, soups, and salads, plus the meat and fish entrées, are reasonably priced. The restaurant is located on a smart stretch of Melrose Avenue just east of Beverly Hills. Its atmosphere resembles a Greenwich Village coffeehouse, much to the delight of Los Angeles' many homesick ex-New Yorkers. But after a few visits to Café Figaro, the magic starts wearing a little thin, and you notice the restaurant's flaws. Despite the promising descriptions on the menu, the food is only so-so and occasionally downright bad. The dining rooms are very noisy and the service is slow.

But at Café Figaro's moderate prices, these faults may not be so annoying after all. And when most other restaurants are closed at 1:00 A.M. and it looks as if you are headed for an all-night coffeeshop, Café Figaro can be a godsend.

$ **MELON'S CLOTHES** *8739 Melrose Avenue. Telephone: 854-3474.*

AND

$ **MELON'S SHOES** *8750 Melrose Avenue. Telephone: 854-7734.*

You're a woman who is visiting Los Angeles and you want to look like an Angeleno fast. What to do? Get a Mercedes® at Budget-Rent-a-Car's deluxe Beverly Hills lot or a Mustang® convertible at Rent-a-Wreck in West Los Angeles, then drive over to Melon's at once. These two stores have the sophisticated yet casual clothes that look so good on trim Los Angeles women and fit the city's pleasant climate so well: skirts and blouses, sweat clothes with hand-painted designs, sneakers in a dozen different colors including hot pink, lime green, and canary yellow, even plastic watchbands in matching shades.

Melon's is not cheap. No store with soft off-white walls, soothing wall-to-wall carpeting, and neon-accented columns could be. But once a woman has got the right car and some Melon's clothes, all she needs is a few days in the sun to pass as a genuine Angeleno.

$ **J. ROBERT SCOTT** *8727 Melrose Avenue. Telephone: 659-4910.*

This "high end" fabrics firm is so sure of itself that its building doesn't even have show windows on the street. Open to the trade only.

$ **DONGHIA** *8715 Melrose Avenue. Telephone: 657-6060.*

This showroom sells very expensive furniture, fabrics, and accessories "to the trade only." Check out the subtly chic gray-brick building with its rounded edges.

$ **COUNTRY FLOORS** *8687 Melrose Avenue. Telephone: 855-1313.*

You may not be planning to redecorate your kitchen or to replace your bathroom floor any time soon. But that shouldn't stop you from visiting Country Floors. Step through the handsome iron gate into the tree-shaded courtyard, then into the store itself, and you will soon realize that Country Floors is an informal gallery as much as a place to buy tiles from France, Italy, the Netherlands, Mexico, and Portugal.

This spacious shop probably has the largest selection of

105

country-style tiles in Los Angeles. So it should not be surprising to see tiles displayed all over the floors, on the walls, on partitions, in fact everywhere except the beamed ceiling. Come to think of it, the storefront is various tiles. What better advertising sign could there be?

At Country Floors, however, you—the general public—can look but not buy; for that, you need your decorator.

$ **DU VIN** *540 North San Vicente Boulevard, just south of Melrose Avenue. Telephone: 855-1161.*

Need a bottle of wine for a friend who has invited you to dinner? Or do you want to have a picnic in one of the local parks or at some scenic promontory in the Hollywood Hills? Stop at Du Vin, which sells a full range of European wines at reasonable prices, plus wonderful cheeses, pâtés, and breads. You're not a wine expert? Don't dismay. Tell one of Du Vin's knowledgeable employees what you like and how much you want to spend, and he will make several good suggestions.

WORD OF ADVICE: If you are planning a picnic, be sure to carry your own corkscrew or ask someone at Du Vin to lift the cork halfway out of your bottle before you leave the store. Nothing will spoil a picnic faster than chipping away at a stubborn cork with one of your car keys.

$ **VERMILLION** *553 North San Vicente Boulevard, corner of Melrose Avenue. Telephone: 659-9180.*

Vermillion sells "high end" furniture and accessories, which are often so "in" today that they might be "out" tomorrow.

$ **PACIFIC DESIGN CENTER** *8687 Melrose Avenue, northeast corner of San Vicente Boulevard.*

A building as large as the Pacific Design Center does not really belong in this low-rise, largely residential neighborhood. Yet, to most people, it has become a well-liked local landmark, rather than an offensive behemoth, thanks to Cesar Pelli's carefully thought out as well as somewhat playful design.

The building is covered with blue glass, hence the nickname "the blue whale." From San Vicente Boulevard, the roofline resembles London's Crystal Palace. At night, the lights shine through the glass walls and arched roof, producing an almost-magical Buck Rogers spaceship sight when viewed from the hills to the north or driving down San Vicente Boulevard just below Sunset Boulevard.

Unless furnishings interest you, just admire the blue whale from the street and drive on, because the entire building is filled with interior decorators' retail and wholesale showrooms. But if you are looking for a place to eat, you might want to stop, because the fourth-floor Designer's Club restaurant is open to the public Monday through Friday from 8:00 A.M. to 7:00 P.M., and it has splendid views of the Hollywood Hills.

$ **SAMUEL BASSETT** *8620 Melrose Avenue. Telephone: 652-9945.*

Samuel Bassett's one-story putty-color shop, which has a lovely row of small palms in front, is so tasteful, so discreet-looking that you could drive by the building again and again without really noticing it. But once you know what Bassett sells in his shop, you'll always slow down to see what he has displayed in his large front windows or park your car and find out what's new inside. On one visit, it might be teddy bears that are large enough to sit on. Another time, it could be a nine-foot-high satin cactus. On yet another visit, it is an all-brass bird cage in the shape of Santa Sophia in Istanbul.

According to Bassett, his attractively arranged shop sells "objects of fantasy." But some regulars describe the often-unique merchandise as "toys for adults." Regardless of who is right, this shop is always filled with the unusual, the whimsical, and the expensive. Ever wanted a brass and crystal lamp whose reedlike lights change colors continuously—or an eight-foot-high papier-mâché giraffe to place near one of the larger potted palms in your living room? Now you know where to find them.

$ ▬▬▬ BODHI TREE BOOKS ▬▬▬ *8585 Melrose Avenue. Telephone: 659-1733.*

In Sanskrit, the word *bodhi* means "enlightenment," and quite appropriately most of this shop's books relate to man's attempts to lead a more satisfying inner life, whether that be through Eastern mysticism, philosophy, meditation, celibacy as well as sexuality, attempts to foretell the future through numerology or astrology, even holistic health and vegetarian diets.

The Bodhi Tree occupies two former houses. The store on Melrose Avenue carries new books and some exotic gifts, such as crystals that reportedly hasten the healing process or other pieces of crystal that break the sun's rays into the colors of the rainbow. The other Bodhi Tree store, which faces the side street, stocks the used books, including many sought-after out-of-print titles. For people who seek spiritual enlightenment and would rather listen to the voices of the various masters than read their teachings, the Bodhi Tree also sells tapes of guru's like Mahareshi, Rajnesh, and Ram Das.

Whichever Bodhi Tree store you visit, the atmosphere is quiet, contemplative, and never hurried. An excellent sound system plays soothing music such as Tibetan bells, Irish harps, flutes, and Gregorian chants. You can serve yourself a complimentary cup of herb tea and sit down on one of the benches and read any of the books as long as you please.

✕ ▬▬▬ MELTING POT ▬▬▬ *8490 Melrose Avenue. West Hollywood. Sunday–Thursday, 8:00 A.M. to 11:00 P.M.; Friday–Saturday, 8:00 A.M. to 1:00 A.M. Telephone: 652-8030. Moderate. American Express, MasterCard, and VISA credit cards.*

With its almost-year-round temperate climate, Los Angeles should have dozens of outdoor cafés and restaurants in all price ranges all over town. Sad to say, it does not.

Of the few restaurants with outdoor tables in West Hollywood, one of the best choices is the conveniently located and reasonably priced Melting Pot, which has an indoor dining room as well as a patio. The omelettes, sandwiches, salads, and several-course meat or fish dinners usually are good. The large patio has comfortable tables and chairs where you can linger easily except at peak dining hours. This place would be nearly perfect if the owners could only do something about the noisy traffic on nearby streets during rush hour. They can't. But you can: Pretend you are at a sidewalk café in Paris. Or leave before 4:00 P.M. Or arrive after 6:00 P.M.

[$] **RICHARD MULLIGAN**   *8471 Melrose Avenue. Telephone: 652-0204.*

It's not everyday that you see a wooden statue of a black-and-white cow standing on a Melrose Avenue sidewalk, with a wooden pig resting on its back, and a wooden rooster perched on *its* back. But it's not that often that you find such a comprehensive selection of good country antiques as you will at Richard Mulligan. Don't miss the storefront either. It's painted to look like a giant black-and-white cow.

[$] **ART AND ARCHITECTURE BOOKS OF THE TWENTIETH CENTURY**   *8375 Melrose Avenue. Telephone: 655-5348.*

Want to read up on the Los Angeles art scene? Or learn more about the city's modern buildings than any general-interest guidebook can tell you? This living-room-size shop has hundreds of books about twentieth-century art and architecture, including several-year-old titles that you won't find at most other bookstores. As an added plus, the salespeople are quite knowledgeable about the books they are selling, and this store also has magazines from all over the world.

$ ■ PARACHUTE ■ *8215 Melrose Avenue. Telephone: 651-0177.*

This is the West Coast outpost for Parachute, which also has shops in Montreal, Miami, New York City's SoHo district, and Toronto. Manufactured in Canada, Parachute's men's and women's clothing have a certain look: loose fitting—they called it "oversized," big-shouldered, and often Oriental-inspired. Not everyone likes Parachute's particular sense of style, but you can't deny that it is very distinctive and *au courant*.

■ THE IMPROVISATION ■ *8162 Melrose Avenue at Crescent Heights. Telephone: 651-2583. Cover charge and minimum.*

Los Angeles has any number of comedy clubs, and The Improvisation is one of the best and most enduring. Showtime is 8:30 P.M., except for Friday and Saturday when the shows begin at 8:00 P.M. and 10:30 P.M. Call The Improv on Monday, and they usually can tell you who is performing for the rest of the week. Don't be surprised one night if someone like Bette Midler, Richard Pryor, or Joan Rivers shows up for an unannounced performance.

On Sundays, you can hear jazz in the back room at The Improv, and on Mondays, they clear away some of the tables in the restaurant and play dance music. The restaurant? Yes, The Improv serves Italian cuisine, including two dozen kinds of pizza. The restaurant is open from noon to 1:30 A.M., Monday through Friday, and from 6:00 P.M. to 1:30 A.M., Saturday and Sunday. Drinks are two-for-the-price-of-one from 4:00 P.M. to 7:00 P.M., Monday through Friday.

LEFT: *Ma Maison, 8368 Melrose Avenue.*

RIGHT: *On trendy Melrose Avenue, even a used clothing store becomes a design statement.*

Melrose Avenue, seen through the window of Aardvark's used-clothing store.

TOP: *Bungalow at Melrose Hill*
trict. RIGHT: *The Pacific Design*
...ter at the northeast corner of
...lrose Avenue and San Vicente
Boulevard. When you see this
...ooming building, you'll know
...hy it's called "the Blue Whale."

TOP: *The Doheny family's Greystone mansion was the grandest house ever built in Beverly Hills, costing $4,000,000 in the late 1920s. But this looming Gothic mansion was the setting for a surprising scandal.* BOTTOM: *View from the Beverly Hills Hotel looking east in 1915.*

$ **FAIRE LA CUISINE/COOKSTORE** *8112 Melrose Avenue. Telephone: 653-1464.*

AND

✗ **FAIRE LA CUISINE/RESTAURANT** *8112 Melrose Avenue. Monday, noon to 3:00 P.M.; Tuesday—Saturday, noon to 3:00 P.M. and 6:30 P.M. to 10:30 P.M.; Sunday, 11:00 A.M. to 3:00 P.M. Telephone: 653-1464. Moderate—expensive. American Express, MasterCard, and VISA credit cards.*

Do you have mixed feelings about visiting gourmet cookstores because you see all those exquisite gadgets and foods, then get hungry but find that the only convenient restaurant is a coffeeshop? Visit Faire la Cuisine and worry no more.

Malcolm and Jeannine Levinthal started Faire la Cuisine as a cookstore, and they sell everything that you need for a French country-style kitchen: pots and pans, utensils, dishes, glassware, as well as tablecloths, placemats, and napkins. Faire la Cuisine also has an unusual selection of gourmet ingredients, such as pine nuts, goat cheeses, sweet Normandy butter, extra-virgin olive oil, and fruit and balsamic vinegars, even candied violets. Just imagine what your food-loving friends will think of that touch on top of dessert.

In 1982 Faire la Cuisine opened its own restaurant, which is located on the rear terrace, just beyond the tempting flower stalls. In its carefully planned casualness, this gardenlike restaurant typifies the Southern California spirit with the profusion of bougainvillea against the latticework walls, the you're-half-indoors-half-outdoors latticework roof, the soft red-brick floor, and the bentwood chairs and circular Italian marble-top tables.

As you would expect, the meals are wonderful, with a typically California emphasis on the finest ingredients, such as organically raised chickens, delicately smoked Petrossian salmon, or smoked duck and quail from Northern California, which are simply prepared and beautifully served with the freshest possible local vegetables. The attention to details even extends to the table water. Faire la Cuisine won't use the foul-tasting stuff that

111

flows out of the tap in Los Angeles. Instead, they serve perfectly chilled Evian mineral water.

For lunch, you can try one of chef Robert Puchol's salads, such as the chicken with spinach and pine nuts in a homemade lemon mayonnaise sauce, the prawns and French beans in a dill-mustard sauce, or the pasta with salami, provolone, and pimientos. Or you simply might want a bowl of the soup of the day, and the assortment of cold meats and pâtés.

For dinner, you can put together a fine à la carte meal consisting of one of those salads, an appetizer like smoked quail with endive and watercress or pasta stuffed with ricotta and spinach in a delicate cream sauce, and one of the half dozen meat and fish entrées, which vary depending on what looked best at the market earlier that day. If sweet Belon oysters are available, chef Puchol might poach and serve them on seaweed. If he has been able to obtain some venison, he might prepare this rich game with a red wine sauce and chestnuts.

Desserts, of course, are great, whether you select the ice cream, fresh fruits, varied pastries, or marquise au chocolat, which is a slice of chocolate mousse in a crème anglaise sauce that tastes far better than it translates into words. The California wine list, likewise, is a marvel, with some six- and seven-year-old vintages that oenophiles rarely find in a new restaurant. About the only disappointment you encounter eating at Faire la Cuisine is admiring some of the gourmet ingredients in the cookstore, then seeing what the kitchen can do with them and knowing that you'd have a difficult time duplicating the tasty results.

$ **FRED SEGAL** *8100 Melrose Avenue. Telephone: 651-4129.*

If the Fred Segal store didn't exist, somebody would have had to invent it. Otherwise half of West Hollywood's fashion-conscious young men and women would not know where to buy their clothes. From Melrose Avenue, Fred Segal looks like a medium-size store. But from the spacious parking lot in the rear, it resembles a small high-style shopping center, consisting of different boutiques for men's and women's sportswear, luggage, shoes, infants' apparel, even greeting cards and stationery.

The largest—and busiest—part of Fred Segal's is the sportswear shop, which is filled with vast stocks of colorful T-shirts and dress shirts, corduroy pants and contemporary-styled jeans, even some almost-one-of-a-kind items like a studded leather vest with gold chain-mail shoulder inserts. The shoppers are obviously having fun here, and if their energy doesn't put you in the same mood, the booming rock music will pick you up and carry you along.

On the second floor, the music—and the ambience—is quite different. This part of Fred Segal's carries drop-dead men's clothes by Giorgio Armani, Jhane Barnes, Alexander Julian, and Kansai, to name but some of the top designers. Need a $460 pair of butter-soft leather pants by Armani? Or a vaguely intimidating $600 black silk suit? You've come to the right place.

$ **ARON'S RECORD SHOP** *7725 Melrose Avenue. Telephone: 653-8170.*

Everyone has records that they no longer play. And everyone recalls some older releases that they would love to own but don't know where to find. In either case, Aron's is the place to go, because they buy back old records and have literally thousands of hard-to-find releases in stock, ranging from classical to punk to jazz. Aron's carries a full stock of new records as well.

✗ **GELATI PER TUTTI** *7653 Melrose Avenue. Telephone: 653-8970.*

Everyone has his or her favorite ice cream shop, and for many Angelenos the first choice is Gelati Per Tutti. What's so special about this place? First, they don't add any air to the ice cream, making it incredibly dense and rich tasting. A little truly goes a long way. Second, what fantastic flavors! Not just vanilla flecked with vanilla bean and the darkest imaginable chocolate, but amaretto, expresso, and zambia, among many others. Now if this pretty pastel-colored shop only had some tables and chairs plus some coffees to wash down the butterfat, the Gelati Per Tutti experience would be perfect.

$ **FLIP** *7607 Melrose Avenue. Telephone: 651-0280.*

On weekends, the only word to describe Flip is "frantic." This large shop is so popular that any day now you expect to see a crowd lined up at the front door, waiting to get in. Once you do walk inside, you are carried away by the enthusiasm of the young men and women who are busily searching through rack after rack of clothes or the equally youthful employees who seem ready to start dancing to the loud music at any moment.

Alice Wolf opened this store three years ago after successfully running three other Flips in England. More than half the merchandise is high-style used clothing; Alice manufactures the rest, all of which carry the Flip name or logo. Gucci, Lacoste, Louis Vuitton, watch out. Here comes Flip.

TOMMY TANG'S SIAMESE CAFE *7473 Melrose Avenue. Monday–Thursday, 10:30 A.M. to 11:00 P.M.; Friday, 11:30 A.M. to midnight; Saturday, 5:00 P.M. to midnight. Telephone: 651-1810. Inexpensive. All major credit cards.*

When Tommy Tang left the kitchen at Chan Dara in Hollywood and opened his own restaurant on the trendiest stretch of Melrose Avenue, more than 500 of his friends and fans showed up for opening night. Why? Because Tang is one of Los Angeles' most accomplished Thai chefs, indeed "the best Thai chef in America" according to the *Bangkok Post,* and he subtly adapts his country's cuisine to American palates.

With his deft touch, Tang prepares appetizers like spicy fried wonton or *mee krob,* a variety of hot and sour or vegetable soups, fried rice and noodle dishes containing meat or shrimp, and several fiery curries. The menu thoughtfully designates various dishes as mild, spicy, or very spicy.

In addition to this usual Thai restuarant fare, Tang also makes some imaginative offerings; for instance, the tasty house salad, which is chicken and hard-boiled egg with peanut dressing, or *yum yai* salad, which consists of shrimp and chicken with romaine lettuce in sweet lemon-egg dressing. Vegetable lovers will rejoice at Tang's baby corn and mushroom plate, the broccoli and bean sprouts with oyster sauce, and the hot and spicy bamboo shoots that are wisely served with cooling mint leaves.

In the section of the menu called "Meat with Veggies," guests can even construct their own beef, chicken, pork, or shrimp entrées which can be prepared with a dozen different vegetables and sauces, such as mushrooms and oyster sauce, green beans with chili sauce, or ginger, onion, and black bean sauce.

Considering Tommy Tang's reasonable prices, you would expect his restaurant to have that familiar low-budget Oriental décor: fluorescent lights, formica-topped tables, linoleum floor, and a garish color scheme. Not so. With its off-white walls and soft pink tablecloths, Provençale furniture, and several comfortable dining areas which face the side street or a pleasant courtyard, Tommy Tang's looks better than many restaurants at twice the price. This is a real find. Enjoy.

$ **ILIFFILI GOURMET NUTS** *7461 Melrose Avenue. Telephone: 651-4104.*

Iliffili (pronounced: ily-fillies) has been open for more than forty years, and when you try the nuts at this small shop, you will know why. Rich-tasting walnuts. Delicate filberts. Sweet-flavored almonds. Some of the finest peanuts you've ever eaten.

Ask Marjorie and Gordon Sando how they achieve such high quality year after year, and they will be pleased to tell you: Start with the finest possible nuts, then patiently roast them in small batches. This explanation sounds so simple that the Sandos' years of experience and obvious love for what they are doing must have some effect on the final results. The store also sells dried fruits and homemade preserves.

HISTORY BUFFS TAKE NOTE: If Iliffili isn't too busy, ask Marjorie Sando what Melrose Avenue was like fifty or sixty years ago. As a little girl, she moved into the neighborhood with her family in 1923, having just arrived in Los Angeles from Kansas City, and she can tell you that Melrose Avenue was a dirt road that ended at Fairfax Avenue and can describe how she and her friends chased rabbits across the empty fields in the neighborhood.

CITY CAFE   *7407½ Melrose Avenue. Monday–Saturday, 10:00 A.M. to 1:00 A.M. Telephone: 658-7495. Moderate–expensive. MasterCard and VISA credit cards.*

The City Café was one of 1982's most welcome additions to the increasingly sophisticated Melrose Avenue restaurant scene. Wedged into a long and narrow storefront, this restaurant is decorated in a chic part-punk/part-1950s look with black marble-topped tables, chrome and black plastic chairs, hanging high-tech lamps, and gray industrial carpeting. The art display on the subtly flecked pink walls changes frequently, no doubt to the relief of some regular patrons.

But it's the food, not the décor or the art, which brings people back to the City Café again and gain, at all times of day until 1:00 A.M. To begin with, chef Susan Feniger has a sensitive eye for detail. The vinaigrette dressing for the dinner salad, for instance, includes fragrant sesame oil. The bottles of mineral

116

water are properly chilled so that they don't have to be served with ice cubes made from the often-foul city water.

Almost without exception, Susan Feniger's meals put some more pretentious restaurants to shame. Between 6:00 P.M. and 10:00 P.M., Monday through Thursday, and until 11:00 P.M. on Friday and Saturday, the dinner specials might include light, almost fluffy potato gnocchis (or dumplings) made to order and served in a Parmesan cream sauce, fried Brie with *coulis* of tomato, or rigatoni stuffed with sausage mousse in a cream sauce. The evening's entrées might be roast leg of rabbit stuffed with herbs, a cold smoked chicken salad that is filled with tiny pieces of sliced vegetables and pineapple, Portuguese mussel and cockle stew, or Koenigsberger Klopse (ground veal balls served on fresh pasta with a caper and cream sauce).

But the dinner specials are only one part of the City Café's delights. All day long, you can order wonderful salads, pâtés, and sandwiches, plus more than a dozen desserts, such as walnut-caramel torte, éclairs, fruit tartes, pithivier with cream, which you can pick out from the pastry case. And you can wash down these sinful desserts with equally good coffee, espresso, cappuccino, or café au lait, made from French beans which are delivered to the restaurant every week.

The City Café attracts a "with-it" crowd in its twenties, thirties, and forties. Join them for dinner, which often is crowded and noisy, or perhaps better yet, for quieter and more relaxed late lunch or an afternoon snack while you are exploring all the nearby shops along Melrose Avenue.

$\boxed{\$}$ **SOAP PLANT**   *7400 Melrose Avenue. Telephone: 651-5587.*

Do you remember those marvelous plastic glasses with the oversized bloodshot eyes that disconcertingly dangled in midair on coiled slinkies whenever you tilted your head forward? You

117

can still find these 1950s relics at the Soap Plant, together with other camp treasures, such as a featherless rubber chicken that you can hang from the overhang pan rack in your kitchen, a "bug gun" which shoots a whirling—and hopefully lethal—plastic disc at offending airborne insects, or the "Pop-Up Washington, D.C.," which is a large card that produces an erect Washington Monument and Lincoln Memorial whenever it is opened.

True to its name, this funky and cluttered store also sells a wide variety of soaps, perfumes, and aromatic oils. You can also find an astonishing variety of funny, offbeat, even downright disgusting greeting cards and postcards that usually aren't carried in the more high-style card and stationery shops.

$ COWBOYS AND POODLES

7379 Melrose Avenue. Telephone: 653-3553.

With a name like Cowboys and Poodles, this shop is sure to attract plenty of curious lookers, at least for one visit. But serious shoppers return again and again to Cow-Poo, as the store is known among Melrose Avenue cognoscenti, because this thrift-store-turned-boutique probably has the largest selection of never-before-worn 1950s clothing in Los Angeles. Want a pair of white bucks that would make Pat Boone weep with envy? Come to Cowboys and Poodles. Need a pair of skin-tight aqua pedal-pushers and matching flats? Try Cow-Poo. Is your life incomplete without a pair of rhinestone-studded hot-pink sunglasses to match your tail-finned 1958 Chrysler convertible? Cow-Poo is the answer.

As if all these clothes weren't enough to complete the illusion, Cowboys and Poodles even looks as if it is right out of the 1950s with its period display cases, chairs, and hanging lamps, which undoubtedly will be the antiques of the future. Maybe they already are.

$ **SIGN OF THE TIMES**   *Bud's Barber Shop, 7023 Melrose Avenue. Telephone: 937-9144.*

Although some of today's avant-garde young men claim to have rediscovered the "flat top" haircut and other closely cropped 1950s styles, the folks at Bud's Barber Shop might disagree. They never gave up on the 1950s look, as you can see from the weather-worn sign above their shop which says "flat tops and contour styling." The sign is illustrated by a crudely painted picture of a man with one of these 1950s styles. But will the young men who like the 1950s look come to a barbershop which is the real 1950s thing complete with massive old-fashioned chairs and the long unshielded fluorescent light tubes over the mirrors?

ROSSMORE AVENUE SIDE TRIP

If you want to see how drastically Los Angeles neighborhoods sometimes differ from block to block, turn right on Rossmore Avenue. Gone are all the gas stations, nondescript shops, and rundown apartment buildings that line the nearby stretch of Melrose Avenue. Once you pass the imposing Spanish-style Christ the King Roman Catholic Church at the curve one block south of Melrose, Rossmore Avenue becomes a dignified tree-lined boulevard with handsome, often 1920s and 1930s apartment buildings on either side.

As you drive south on Rossmore, don't miss the Ravenswood on your left at 570 North Rossmore, a zigzag Moderne 1930s building, which was the long-time home of sultry Mae West. Just down the street, you will also see the vaguely Spanish, vaguely French château El Royale Apartments at 450 North Rossmore, which at various times has been the home of actor George Raft, Columbia Pictures czar Harry Cohn, and actor William Frawley, who played Fred in television's "I Love Lucy" show. John F. Kennedy stayed at the El Royale during the 1960 Democratic convention in Los Angeles.

After the El Royale, turn around and head north on Rossmore, back the way you just came. Drive carefully. This is a major north-to-south thoroughfare and traffic moves quickly. If you feel curious, turn right on Rosewood Avenue and explore Arden Boulevard, which is parallel to Rossmore and the next street to the east. You won't see any movie stars' homes or astonishing architecture here, just dozens of scarcely changed middle-class houses from the 1920s, which look as if they were located in a small town rather than in the middle of Los Angeles.

LUCY'S EL ADOBE CAFE   *5536 Melrose Avenue. Monday–Saturday, 11:30 A.M. to 11:30 P.M. Telephone: 462-9421. Moderate. MasterCard and Visa credit cards.*

Lucy's El Adobe Café looks like another simple Mexican restaurant in this increasingly Mexican part of Hollywood. But it's not. Lucy's has become a Los Angeles restaurant landmark, just like Perino's or Scandia, except that it serves an outwardly less elegant clientele. To be more specific, when Jerry Brown was governor of California, Lucy's was one of his favorite hangouts, and he sometimes took Linda Ronstadt here for dinner while they were dating.

If you go to Lucy's probably all you'll see are people who work at some of the nearby studios. Then again, you never know who might show up.

ORIGINAL 1926 PARAMOUNT PICTURES GATE   *5451 Marathon Avenue. Visible looking up Bronson Avenue from Santa Monica Boulevard.*

If you remember the 1950 film *Sunset Boulevard*, in which Gloria Swanson plays Norma Desmond, a once-renowned but now almost-forgotten and half-mad silent star, then you will recognize the original arched Spanish-style gate at Paramount Pictures, which figures prominently in one scene of the movie. Halfway through *Sunset Boulevard,* Norma Desmond wants to make her comeback, and on a whim one day she decides to visit Paramount, which was her former studio. When Norma arrives at Paramount in her vintage Isotta Fraschini, the guard will not let the car past the gate, because she does not have an appointment and he does not recognize her. Only when an older guard sees that it is Norma Desmond and a throng of admirers quickly gathers, do the elaborate wrought-iron gates open majestically and her car slowly enters the lot.

HISTORICAL FOOTNOTE: In *Sunset Boulevard,* one-time director Erich von Stroheim played Max von Meyerling, who was Norma Desmond's combination butler-manservant-chauffeur. But in reality, Von Stroheim could not drive. For this dramatic scene at Paramount, the Isotta Fraschini was towed into the studio on a cable.

 WESTERN COSTUME COMPANY *5335 Melrose Avenue. Telephone: 469-1451.*

Who do you want to be today? Scarlett O'Hara? Tarzan? Betty Boop? Bugs Bunny? Look no further than Western Costume, which has been renting clothes to nearby studios and anyone else since the 1920s.

LOS ANGELES UNIFORM EXCHANGE *5239 Melrose Avenue. Telephone: 469-3965.*

Is dressing up like a marine drill sergeant, a British Navy sailor, or a California Highway Patrolman your thing? Or would you like to see how you look in these uniforms? This store probably has the largest stock of American and European uniforms for sale in Los Angeles.

121

✗ **MAX HENRY'S**   *5200 Melrose Avenue. Monday–Thursday, 10:00 A.M. to 10:00 P.M.; Friday–Saturday, 10:00 A.M. to 11:00 P.M. Telephone: 460-6306. Inexpensive. MasterCard and VISA credit cards.*

Max Henry's serves hearty deli sandwiches and German specialties like Sauerbraten, smoked pork chops, or Schnitzel, plus more than one hundred different beers from all over the world. Paramount Studios is across the street, and the restaurant is often jammed at lunch.

ARCHITECTURAL CONTRASTS SIDE TRIP

As you head east on Melrose Avenue, turn left on Manhattan Place, which is one block west of Western Avenue. Proceed one block to Marathon Avenue, and examine the Jardinette Apartments at 5128 Marathon. Can you guess when this five-story apartment building was completed? From the look of its squared massing, the poured concrete walls, and the rectangular bands of metal-framed windows, you probably would guess sometime in the 1960s. And you would be wrong. The actual date is 1927.

How could that be possible? Weren't Los Angeles architects and builders hopelessly infatuated with the Spanish and Olde English styles in the 1920s? Yes, but not *every* architect was caught up in historical revival styles at the time. A few were experimenting with the International Style or what many people call "modern architecture," which had just originated with Le Corbusier, Walter Gropius, and Mies van der Rohe in Europe.

Richard Neutra, shortly after arriving in Los Angeles in 1925, designed the U-shaped 30,000-square-foot Jardinette Apartments, which contained fifty-five apartments arranged around the rectangular front courtyard. When the building was completed in 1927, it was widely hailed as one of the first International-Style buildings in America, and Neutra's career was off to a promising start.

To see a very different 1920s apartment building, drive several hundred feet east on Marathon Avenue to Western Avenue. Turn left on Western and proceed north. One block north of Santa Monica Boulevard, turn left on Virginia Avenue. Go one block, then turn right on St. Andrew's Place. When you reach Lexington Avenue, turn left. At 5616 Lexington, you come to the ancient Egyptian-style Ahmed Apartments, completed in 1925, just two years before Neutra's avant-garde Jardinette Apartments. Return to St. Andrew's Place, turn left and head one block north, and turn left on La Mirada Avenue. The aptly named Egyptian-style Karnak Apartments stand at 5617 La Mirada.

To return to Melrose Avenue, head south on St. Andrew's Place, turn left on Santa Monica Boulevard, proceed one block and turn right on Western Avenue. When you reach Marathon Avenue, which is one block before Melrose, turn left, thereby avoiding the difficult turn onto Melrose from Western and entering the next destination, Melrose Hill.

MELROSE HILL SIDE TRIP

If you want to discover one of the best-kept secrets in the Hollywood "flats," continue eastward on Marathon for two blocks, then turn left on Melrose Hill North, which ends in a cul de sac. Now you are in the middle of the Melrose Hill district, a three-block, forty-five-house enclave which shows what most working-class Los Angeles neighborhoods looked like after World War I. (If you skipped the Architectural Contrasts side trip, and continued eastward on Melrose, simply turn left on Oxford Avenue, which is one block east of Western Avenue. After one block, you will come to Marathon, when you turn right and soon come to Melrose Hill North.)

Melrose Hill's modest one- and two-family houses date from

the late nineteenth century to 1923. Nothing has been built in the district since that date! Only a handful of these houses have been changed outside. Some are classic Southern California bungalows. Others are Dutch Colonials, mock-Tudor cottages, or Spanish haciendas in miniature. Everywhere you look are well-tended front lawns behind white picket fences, sixty-year-old trees, and a profusion of flowers, especially roses. And thanks to the cul de sacs on Melrose Hill North and Melrose Hill West, which leads off Melrose Hill North, through-traffic is non-existent, and you can actually hear insects buzzing through the air and birds singing in the trees.

Why has Melrose Hill remained an attractive and stable neighborhood when so much of the Hollywood "flats" has become characterless commercial sprawl and apartment buildings in various stages of decay? Because Melrose Hill North, Melrose Hill West, and the adjacent block of Marathon Avenue are the only part of the Hollywood "flats" still zoned for one- and two-family houses, instead of apartment buildings. With real estate developers effectively barred from the neighborhood, working- and middle-class families still own—and occupy—nearly all the houses. Over the years, these residents have earned enough money to maintain their homes, yet not enough to drastically modernize the exteriors. Now young professionals are moving into Melrose Hill, because they like the area's unspoiled architecture. its central location, its feeling of peace, and its genuine neighborliness.

$ **DESIGN RESOURCE** *5160 Melrose Avenue. Telephone: 465-9235.*

Twenty years ago, you would never have found a store which sold cast-iron caryatids, ornamental ceiling rosettes, or Doric columns in wood. But with the current interest in historic architecture, stores like Design Resource have opened across the nation. This one should not be missed, whether you are a post-Modernist architect who is sticking eighteenth- and nineteenth-century details onto otherwise contemporary buildings, a strict preservationist who is restoring a turn-of-the-century mansion, or simply someone who wants to place a gargoyle on one wall of the living room.

BACKGROUND

Beverly Hills is the classic overnight rags-to-riches story. At the turn of the century, its reputation had nothing to do with movie stars, millionaires, and mansions. Instead, most of present-day Beverly Hills north of Wilshire Boulevard was the Rancho Rodeo de las Aguas (or the "gathering of waters"), and it was known for its beans, acres and acres of beans.

Only a few dozen people lived in Beverly Hills, and not one was a millionaire, just Mexican farm workers in a cluster of shacks along unpaved Santa Monica Boulevard, families like the Benedicts and the Willfongs nestled in the hills and canyons above the bean fields, and a Chinese man named Seng, who cultivated a vegetable farm in a little valley called "Chinaman Canyon" in the hills near present-day Schuyler Road.

Just after the turn of the century, big things began to happen in Beverly Hills. Oil had been discovered immediately to the east

126

in the workingmen's village of Sherman (now West Hollywood), and an oil syndicate headed by Charles Canfield, Burton Green, and Max Whittier paid $670,000 for the Rancho Rodeo de las Aguas, hoping to find exploitable deposits under the bean fields. In 1905 and early 1906, the syndicate drilled more than thirty wells but didn't find any appreciable oil except in the south-western edge of the property near today's Century City office towers.

Canfield, Green, and Whittier had spent too much money for this property to continue raising beans. So they decided to turn the ranch into a real estate development, whose boundaries started at Wilshire Boulevard on the south, Whittier Drive on the west, the hills above Sunset Boulevard to the north, and Doheny Drive to the east, in all, an area approximately one and a half by two miles.

Although six miles of barley fields, orange groves, cattle ranches, and oilfields separated the bean ranch from the west-ernmost edge of Los Angeles, Canfield, Green, and Whittier had high hopes for their venture. The Los Angeles real estate market was thriving, and the ranch occupied a particularly favorable spot, thirty-five minutes from downtown Los Angeles and twenty minutes from beach towns like Santa Monica and Venice by way of the trolley, which ran along Santa Monica Boulevard and stopped in Beverly Hills at the present-day corner of Canon Drive. The foothills of the Santa Monica Mountains formed a striking backdrop to the bean-field-filled flats and offered fine views of the Pacific Ocean.

Having formed the Rodeo Land and Water Company to sell lots to families who would build homes, Canfield, Green, and Whittier named their development Beverly Hills after the town of Beverly Farms, Massachusetts. Burton Green, so the story goes, was a great admirer of President William Howard Taft, and he thought up the name after reading that Taft had visited Beverly Farms.

After opening Crescent, Canon, Beverly, and Rodeo drives through the bean fields between Santa Monica and Sunset bou-levards, Rodeo Land and Water built four or five model homes, including one still surviving at 515 North Canon Drive. In January 1907, the first lots went on the market. One-acre properties along Sunset Boulevard were $800 to $1,000. The 80-by-200-foot lots in the blocks nearest to Santa Monica Boulevard cost $300 to $400. For the first few years, Rodeo Land and Water offered a 10 percent discount if the purchaser paid cash and another 10 percent if construction on the lot started within six months. The second discount, hopefully, would encourage families to build homes and give Beverly Hills a settled look which would attract more buyers.

By the mid-teens, Beverly Hills was starting to acquire an elegant suburban look. The bean fields in the flats below Sunset Boulevard were giving way to dozens of large, comfortable homes and more newly opened streets. A neighborhood shopping district was emerging on several streets, like Rodeo Drive, just below Santa Monica Boulevard. The Mission-style Beverly Hills Hotel, which opened at Sunset Boulevard and Crescent Drive in 1911, was the physical focus of the community, as well as the one place where local residents could go out for dinner or watch the "flickers." Most important, Beverly Hills' population was growing, and it reached 634 in 1920, quite a jump over the 250 residents the community somewhat dubiously claimed in order to become an independent city in 1914. Many of these residents were retired East Coast or Middle Western businessmen, who moved to Southern California for its temperate climate. Others were successful professionals and businessmen who took the trolley along Santa Monica Boulevard to their offices in downtown Los Angeles.

Shortly after the First World War, Beverly Hills' days as a quiet and genteel Los Angeles suburb ended forever. The crucial event was Douglas Fairbanks, Sr.'s purchase of a hunting lodge in the then-empty and rustic foothills behind the Beverly Hills Hotel. With the help of his studio art director, Fairbanks remodeled the lodge into a handsome pseudo-Tudor home, which stood on a ridge overlooking Benedict Canyon. After Mary Pickford married Douglas Fairbanks, Sr., in 1920, she moved onto this 14-acre estate, which the press promptly dubbed "Pickfair."

In the next few years, Charlie Chaplin, Will Rogers, and Gloria Swanson settled in Beverly Hills, because it offered a comfort-

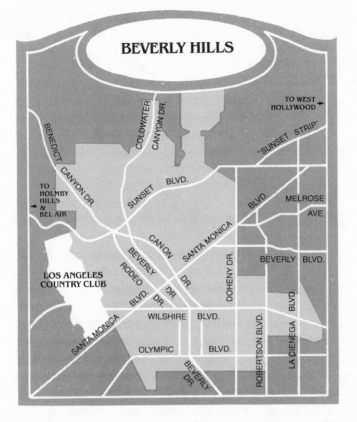

BEVERLY HILLS

able country mood, yet was an easy drive to their Hollywood studios. The movie stars, moreover, felt unwelcome in more centrally located "Society" neighborhoods such as Hancock Park and Windsor Square, and the prejudice against "movie people" even pervaded some of the palm-lined boulevards at the base of the Hollywood Hills.

The presence of internationally acclaimed stars like Fairbanks, Pickford, and Chaplin gave Beverly Hills an image of glamour and wealth, which attracted additional movie stars, producers, and directors, as well as rich businessmen and their families. Sharing in the Southern California boom of the 1920s, Beverly Hills' population jumped from 634 in 1920 to 17,428 in 1930.

Since then, Beverly Hills has been one of the most fashionable, most talked-about communities in Los Angeles, indeed in the entire United States, but with a distinct difference. Unlike other posh suburbs, Beverly Hills has a flamboyant, even reckless image, in part because of the many free-spending stars who were nobodies five or ten years ago and could become just that five or ten years in the future. Where else can you count new Mercedes and Rolls-Royces by the dozens, watch shoppers add tens of thousands of dollars to their charge accounts during a single afternoon, or sit next to your favorite movie star in a restaurant?

BEVERLY HILLS TOUR START: *Sunset Boulevard and Doheny Drive.*

TIME: *Approximately three hours, including stop on Rodeo Drive.*

When you drive west along Sunset Boulevard toward Beverly Hills, you don't have to see a sign in order to know where West Hollywood's raucous Sunset Strip ends and this privileged five-square-mile city begins. Suddenly, the restaurants, shops, rock clubs, and office buildings disappear, and Sunset Boulevard turns into a gently curving thoroughfare with a wide, grassy median running down the center and beautifully landscaped Spanish- and Tudor-style mansions standing far back from the street behind gates.

Sunset Boulevard's unabashed display of wealth is not limited to its mansions. Except for rush hour, when some mere mortals use the street for commuting, Sunset Boulevard probably is filled with more luxury cars than any other place in the world, except perhaps for nearby Rodeo Drive. How many Rolls-Royces can you spot? Don't bother to get excited about Mercedeses and Jaguars. They are too numerous to mention, and anyway many of them are leased, just like most of the Rolls-Royces.

Do you want to see the grandest house ever built in Beverly Hills, indeed the most extravagant residence ever constructed west of the Mississippi River with the exception of William Randolph Hearst's fabled San Simeon? The mansion is called Greystone and it was built by Edward Laurence Doheny, Sr., the Los Angeles oil millionaire who became embroiled in the Teapot

130

Dome scandal in the early 1920s, because he gave Secretary of the Interior Albert Fall a $100,000 bribe in return for secret leases to government oil reserves at Elk Hills and Buena Vista in California.

To see Greystone, turn right on Mountain Drive, which is about a half mile beyond the Beverly Hills city line. When you come to Loma Vista Drive, which is the next intersection, turn right and head uphill, past Doheny Road, until you see the sign on the left for Greystone Park, which is open to the public at no charge every day from 10:00 A.M. to 6:00 P.M. Follow this road up the hill to the parking lot. The mansion is closed to the public, but you can wander through the 16-acre gardens and enjoy the view of Beverly Hills below.

In 1928, Edward Laurence Doheny, Sr., completed Greystone at the then-stupefying cost of $4,000,000. But look what he got for his money. The mansion had fifty-five rooms, totaling 46,504 square feet. Its gray Arizona stone façade, which gave the house its name, was merely a veneer for thick-steel-framed concrete walls. Even the slate roof was reinforced with concrete.

Located on this prominent hillside, where it overlooked the mansions of Beverly Hills' mere millionaires just as medieval castles loomed over the huts of the nobleman's serfs, Greystone was the focal point of a 415-acre ranch, which extended far up the nearby hills. As befitted his thirst for wealth and power, Doheny ran this ranch like his own principality, complete with its own watchmen, water supply, and fire department. The 25 acres, which immediately surrounded the mansion, included a 15,666-square-foot stable, a seven-room gate house, greenhouses, swimming pools, tennis and badminton courts, and two concrete-bottom lakes, not to mention acres and acres of formal gardens and carefully planned "natural" wooded areas.

Edward Laurence Doheny never lived at Greystone. Instead, he gave the house to his only child, Edward Laurence, Jr., or Ned, who moved into the mansion with his wife and five children. But Ned did not enjoy his father's magnificent gift for long. On the evening of February 17, 1929, two muffled gunshots rang out in the house. Afterward Ned Doheny and his secretary, Hugh Plunkett, lay dead in Ned's bedroom suite.

What was going on? According to Doheny family spokesmen, Plunkett had been "highly excited and nervous" in recent months, and Ned was trying to convince him to retire. But this statement did not explain why the two men were dead or what Plunkett had been doing in Ned's bedroom in the first place.

The rumor mills worked overtime, turning out different versions of what had really happened. One story is farfetched, but it is the one that many old-timers believe: Ned Doheny and Hugh Plunkett were lovers, and the family had just found out. Rather than suffer public exposure or, at best, be forced to stop seeing each other, the two men decided to kill themselves. That Saturday night at Greystone, Doheny shot and killed Plunkett, then put the gun to his head and pulled the trigger.

When you leave Greystone Park, return to Sunset Boulevard the same way that you came, and turn right on Sunset, heading west again. Do you remember the "Sheik's House," which attracted nationwide publicity in the late 1970s for its stucco walls painted lime-green, its copper roof, its outdoor urns filled with plastic flowers, and its naked statues, complete with realistic pubic hair, standing on the terrace overlooking Sunset Boulevard? When you pass Alpine Drive, slow down and look to your right. The Sheik is gone. His house burned in a spectacular—and highly suspicious—fire on New Year's Eve, 1980. But you can still see the mansion's scorched walls and the half-collapsed copper roof.

At Rexford Drive, which is the next street, turn left and proceed four blocks until you come to Santa Monica Boulevard, where you turn right. As you drive down Rexford, notice how the houses start out as million-dollar-or-more mansions near Sunset Boulevard but become glorified, albeit half-a-million-dollar bungalows in the block closest to Santa Monica Boulevard.

Every town has a "right side" and a "wrong side" of the tracks, and Beverly Hills is no exception. The dividing line is Santa Monica Boulevard, which runs parallel to a now-unused trolley line. Above Santa Monica Boulevard, or to the north, the streets are solidly residential and expensive, as you have seen on Rexford Drive. Below Santa Monica Boulevard, or to the south, the streets are—and have always been—a mixture of shops, offices, and less expensive houses and apartments.

In the 1930s, the Beverly Hills city fathers installed the narrow greensward along the north side of Santa Monica Boulevard, as it passed through Beverly Hills, in order to protect real estate values "above the tracks." Today, this two-mile-long park is a favorite jogging path, and it even has a cactus garden between Camden and Bedford drives.

Carefully obey traffic laws in Beverly Hills, especially the one which requires that you stop your car for a pedestrian in a crosswalk, even when there is no stoplight or STOP sign. Beverly Hills seems to be crawling with patrol cars, particularly in the vicinity of the police station, which is located in the flamboyant Spanish-style City Hall on the south side of Santa Monica Boulevard between Rexford and Crescent drives. The lovely Italian Renaissance-style post office occupies the next blockfront to the west.

Slow down. Coming up is Rodeo Drive, probably the most talked-about street in America. Fifteen years ago, Rodeo Drive was Beverly Hills' most stylish shopping street, but it was little known outside the community. In the mid-1970s, some of Europe's finest clothing shops and jewelers opened branches on Rodeo Drive, which attracted well-to-do Angelenos and tourists, which in turn led to the opening of more fine shops, and so forth.

For some shoppers, Rodeo Drive is the nearest thing to heaven, and only the rich and the beautiful seem to grace its sidewalks. For other observers, Rodeo Drive is a hopelessly vulgar shrine to conspicuous consumption, and it looks like a shopping mall playing dress-up, where the people are pretending to be something that they aren't.

Although the truth lies somewhere in between, outwardly these three blocks of Rodeo Drive make up one of the most glamorous sections in the world, on a par with upper Madison Avenue in New York, Bond Street in London, and the rue du Faubourg Saint Honoré in Paris. Also, for Angelenos, Rodeo Drive is one place where they get out of their cars for more than one or two errands and can actually walk around for an hour or two. The sidewalks are a people-watcher's paradise. Is that really Zsa Zsa Gabor stepping out of that Rolls-Royce? You bet. And the window-shopping is unbeatable, particularly at night when the brightly lit store windows look like oversized jewel boxes, lined up one after the other.

One important suggestion: Don't confine your wandering just to Rodeo Drive. Check out the shops on "little" Santa Monica Boulevard, Brighton Way, and Dayton Way, which intersect Rodeo Drive. The rents are lower on these side streets, and sometimes the merchants carry more unusual or one-of-a-kind merchandise than the Rodeo Drive stores, which must move large quantities of merchandise every month to meet their higher overheads.

Also, don't forget to walk up and down Wilshire Boulevard at the foot of Rodeo Drive. On either side of the looming Beverly Wilshire Hotel but particularly to the west, you will find Abercrombie and Fitch (at 9424 Wilshire), Bonwit Teller (9536), I. Magnin (9634), Neiman-Marcus (9700), Saks Fifth Avenue (9600), and Tiffany (9502). Note the lovely, classically inspired Moderne architecture of the Magnin and Saks stores, which were built in the late 1930s.

Before you start your shopping foray or vicariously watch others on the prowl, you must park your car somewhere. You have three choices, and each one represents a trade-off between cost and comfort. Starting at the top, you can drop off the car at one of the well-signed valet parking stations along Rodeo Drive, which are open from 9:00 A.M. to 6:00 P.M., Monday through Saturday. Most of the Rodeo Drive shops validate your parking stub, if you make a purchase, and then the charge is only $1.50. Without a store validation, the charge is $5.00, plus the garage fee, which leads to your second option.

Park the car yourself in the reasonably priced municipal garage on the west side of Rodeo Drive just south of Brighton Way. If that garage is full, drive over to one of the nearby streets, which are parallel to Rodeo Drive, and you will probably find a municipal garage with space. Beware of the city-run open lots where attendants park the car for you. The rates are higher than at the park-it-yourself garages.

For the ultimate in frugality, leave your car on one of the residential blocks just north of Santa Monica Boulevard. You will

134

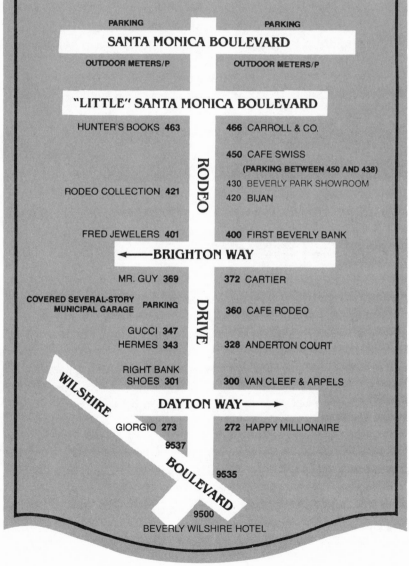

HIGHLIGHTS OF RODEO DRIVE

N.B.: Free two-hour street parking along the residential stretch of Rodeo Drive, north of Santa Monica Boulevard.

PARKING   PARKING

SANTA MONICA BOULEVARD

OUTDOOR METERS/P   OUTDOOR METERS/P

"LITTLE" SANTA MONICA BOULEVARD

HUNTER'S BOOKS **463**   **466** CARROLL & CO.

450 CAFE SWISS

(PARKING BETWEEN 450 AND 438)

430 BEVERLY PARK SHOWROOM

RODEO COLLECTION **421**   **420** BIJAN

RODEO

FRED JEWELERS **401**   **400** FIRST BEVERLY BANK

←—BRIGHTON WAY

MR. GUY **369**   **372** CARTIER

COVERED SEVERAL-STORY MUNICIPAL GARAGE   **PARKING**   **360** CAFE RODEO

DRIVE

GUCCI **347**
HERMES **343**   **328** ANDERTON COURT

RIGHT BANK
SHOES **301**   **300** VAN CLEEF & ARPELS

DAYTON WAY—→

GIORGIO **273**   **272** HAPPY MILLIONAIRE

WILSHIRE

9537

BOULEVARD   **9535**

9500

BEVERLY WILSHIRE HOTEL

have to walk a few minutes to reach Rodeo Drive's shopping stretch, but you will pay nothing. This may be the only time that you find a bargain while shopping on Rodeo Drive. IMPORTANT NOTE: On most of these residential streets, you can park free for two hours, but check the signs along the curb to make sure that you have selected one of these locations.

ANOTHER CAUTION: Rents are so high on Rodeo Drive that shops open and close with disconcerting frequency. Don't be surprised if the shop that you visited several months ago or heard about from a friend no longer exists. If you had your heart set on see-ing that store, check the telephone information directory. Maybe the shop moved to one of the side streets off Rodeo Drive or into West Hollywood, perhaps at Sunset Plaza or on Melrose Avenue.

RODEO DRIVE AND VICINITY HIGHLIGHTS

$ **VICTOR ARWAS GALLERY** *445 North Rodeo Drive. Telephone: 858-0824.*

This is one of the most beautiful shops on Rodeo Drive, and the reason is not the store building or the shop itself, which has soft gray wall-to-wall carpeting, walls, and ceiling. Instead, it is Victor Arwas' amazing selection of richly colored and beautifully crafted Art Nouveau and Art Deco furniture, lamps, glassware, and objets d'art. For the window-shopper, the Victor Arwas Gallery looks even better at night than by day, if that is possible.

$ **GIORGIO** *273 North Rodeo Drive. Telephone: 278-7312.*

It's a toss-up whether Bijan or Giorgio is the best-known shop on Rodeo Drive. Bijan is the most expensive store on the street.

But the white-and-yellow-awninged Giorgio was the star of Judith Krantz's best-selling novel *Scruples,* and unlike Bijan, you won't have to make an appointment to go shopping.

Step inside Giorgio, and you are surrounded by lovely men's and women's clothing and shoes. Although the salesclerks are unusually accommodating and knowledgeable, owner Fred Hayman goes even further to make sure that his customers feel at home: You can play billiards at Giorgio, have a cup of espresso, even order a drink from the bar, and it's all on the house. And if you go on a shopping spree, the ever-gracious Hayman will send you and all your packages back home or to your hotel in his classic Rolls-Royce.

$ **BIJAN** *420 North Rodeo Drive. Telephone: 273-6544.*

With the possible exception of Giorgio down the street, Bijan is the most talked about shop on Rodeo Drive. The store is furnished with French antiques, a $40,000 Persian carpet, and a crystal chandelier. The men's clothes are some of the most expensive in the world: $2,000 suits, $300 shirts, and $100 for a humble necktie. And the store won't let just anyone in the front door. You have to make an appointment or be recognized at the entrance as a big spender.

If all this is appealing, but you're not the type to get a favorable nod from the help, hurry over to Bijan fast for a peek in the windows. Sooner or later, they are going to figure out a way to keep the hoi polloi from peering through the tall, arched windows and smudging the glass.

NATE 'N AL'S *414 North Beverly Drive. Open seven days, 7:30 A.M. to 8:45 P.M. Telephone: 274-0101. Moderate.*

Many of the ex-New Yorkers in Los Angeles spend half their time complaining about their newly adopted city. If it's not the complete dependency on the automobile, it's the smog, the lack of East Coast-style seasons, the superficialty of the locals. But another one of Los Angles' real or imagined faults—the lack of good deli food—is easy to solve. Just join the crowds at Nate 'N Al's. Here homesick New Yorkers can get all the well-prepared chicken soup, matzoh brei, or combination sandwiches that their hearts and appetites desire, plus a good helping of the noisy and upbeat New York deli mood.

Going to Nate 'N Al's is a lot cheaper than catching the next plane to New York. And who knows, you might see one of your favorite stars sitting in one of the booths or picking up some food at the bustling takeout counter. How often does that happen in a New York deli?

 CAFE RODEO   *360 North Rodeo Drive. Open seven days, 7:00 A.M. to 10:00 A.M., 11:30 A.M. to 10:00 P.M. Telephone: 273-0300. Moderate to expensive. All major credit cards. Valet parking.*

One of the best finds on Rodeo Drive has nothing to do with shopping. It's the covered terrace at the Café Rodeo, where you can eat lunch, rest your feet, and enjoy some of the world's best people-watching all at the same time. Do anything to get one of the tables overlooking the sidewalk. Thanks to the protective cover of the arches and the leafy ficus trees, you can see everyone walk by, yet hardly anyone will notice what you are doing.

$ LA FROMAGERIE/THE CHEESE STORE   *419 North Beverly Drive. Telephone: 278-2855.*

You don't need to look for a sign to find La Fromagerie. A hundred feet away, you can smell the ripe, rich aromas of cheeses wafting out the front door of this shop. La Fromagerie has one of the most complete cheese selections in Los Angeles. All are fresh and beautifully arranged: sharp English Cheddars, strong Italian Parmesans, soft French Bries and Camemberts, even California's own delicate goat cheeses, to name a few of the obvious choices. But why pick a cheese that you already know at a store like this? Ask the shop's clerk for a sample of something really good and unusual. Maybe you'll like that better than what you had planned to buy.

Despite its name, La Fromagerie sells pâtés, pastas, breads, mineral waters, and wines. What a wonderful place to put together a superb dinner or a gourmet picnic.

 JURGENSEN'S GROCERY *409 North Beverly Drive. Telephone: 274-8611.*

Movie stars and millionaires have to eat just like the rest of us. But they don't go—or send their maids—to just any supermarket. Quite often, they do their shopping at Jurgensen's, which puts other groceries to shame: The food is not only good-tasting; in the true Beverly Hills tradition, it is good-looking as well—perfect peaches, lovely lamb chops, and the like. The atmosphere is quiet and unhurried, with no shoppers' specials being blared over a loudspeaker here.

 WILLIAMS-SONOMA *438 North Rodeo Drive. Telephone: 274-9127.*

Need a flower-shaped baking mold? An imported French nutmeg grinder? A $750 Italian ice-cream machine? Or do you know someone who does?

Williams-Sonoma is the place to go, because it has one of the most complete selections of gourmet cookware and equipment in Los Angeles. The store also sells those often-elusive ingredients, such as raspberry vinegar, almond and walnut oils, and spices from Provence, all arranged as handsomely as the designer clothes in the nearby boutiques. If you see something that you like but don't want to buy it at once, you can also order it from the Williams-Sonoma catalog at a later date. Pick one up and put yourself on their mailing list before you leave.

✘ **JACOPO'S** *490 North Beverly Drive. Sunday–Thursday, 11:30 A.M. to midnight; Friday and Saturday, 11:30 A.M. to 2:00 A.M. Telephone: 858-6446. Inexpensive.*

At almost any hour of the day or night, Jacopo's is jammed. But what's this small restaurant doing right? It's not the ambience of its noisy, cramped dining room or the small red-brick building, which stands next to the now-abandoned railroad tracks along Santa Monica Boulevard. And it's not the very ordinary spaghetti-and-meatball-type pasta dishes. No, the reason for Jacopo's popularity is its pizza, made with fresh dough crusts, plenty of cheese, and thick, flavorful tomato sauce, plus dozens of toppings.

✘ **BROOKLYN'S FAMOUS PIZZA** *9383 Wilshire Boulevard. Sunday, noon to midnight; Monday–Thursday, 11:00 A.M. to midnight; Friday and Saturday, 11:00 A.M. to 1:00 A.M. Telephone: 858-1303. Inexpensive.*

A pizza joint just a few minutes' walk from Rodeo Drive and the Beverly Wilshire Hotel? Yes, and its crunchy, thin-crust pizzas consistently rank among Los Angeles' very best, according to the local critics. Looking like dozens of New York pizza parlors, Brooklyn's Famous doesn't offer much in the way of creature comforts, other than a few tables and chairs. Instead, take the pizza back to your suite at the Beverly Wilshire or eat it in your Rolls-Royce. You won't be the first.

$ | **BEVERLY PARK SHOWROOM** | *430 North Rodeo Drive.*

What is the most expensive shop on Rodeo Drive? Fred? Bijan? Gucci? No, it is the showroom for Beverly Park, an estates-only development in the hills one mile north of the Beverly Hills Hotel. Like the original sections of Beverly Hills and Bel Air, Beverly Park is a sensitively planned, spare-no-costs community. There are only seventy-six estate sites on this 320-acre hilltop property, as well as a Gothic gatehouse, guards at each of the three entrances, and winding streets flanked by garden malls.

Even if you are not in the market for a $1.5 million-and-up homesite, step through this showroom's 20-foot-high bronze and beveled glass front doors. You'll see a detailed 6-by-20-foot-long model of Beverly Park, which shows famous Beverly Hills estates as if they were located on Beverly Park lots. There is a ten-minute videotape that begins with aerial shots of Rodeo Drive and the Beverly Hills Hotel, before it lands you at one entrance to Beverly Park for a drive along its roads and a visit to some of its homesites.

But the Beverly Park showroom's *pièce de résistance* is the EPCOT-style video "touch screen." Here you can "visit" the greatest estates in Beverly Hills, Holmby Hills, and Bel Air, and because the screen is " interactive," you decide what you want to view and for how long.

At first, you see a map of Beverly Hills , Holmby Hills, and Bel Air. Are you interested in Holmby Hills? Touch that portion of the screen and a detailed map of Holmby Hills appears—with a dozen dots, each one representing that community's greatest residences. Do you want to see Hugh Hefner's Playboy Mansion? Press that dot. Suddenly an aerial of the estate appears. Do you want to get a closer look at the front of the house, the swimming pool, even the entrance to the famed stereo and Jacuzzi-equipped grotto? Touch that portion of the aerial and you're there.

The Beverly Park showroom is open late seven days a week.

$ **RODEO COLLECTION** *421 North Rodeo Drive.*

Just when Rodeo Drive regulars were becoming just the slightest bit bored with strolling in and out of Bijan, Giorgio, or Gucci, Persian developer Daryoush Mahboudi opened the five-level Rodeo Collection, which puts most of the street to shame for sheer extravagance and architectural excess.

Take the underground garage—excuse me, the "auto reception area." No dimly lit concrete ramp and grimy cinderblock walls here. Instead, the driveway is a dark shade of red brick, laid in an interesting pattern. The brick walls are another attractive red color. When you leave your car with the uniformed parking attendants at the bottom of the ramp, the softly lit reception area has red-brick and gold-veined white-marble walls, splashing fountains with nineteenth-century French statues, and all kinds of ornamental plants, including potted palms, ferns, even orchids.

After such a dramatic automobile entrance, the Rodeo Collection itself could be an anticlimax. It's not. After taking the escalators or the circular glass elevator up to the first shopping level, you step into the soaring central courtyard where you are surrounded by more handsome brick, gold-veined white marble, and plants. Although the Rodeo Collection building combines too many architectural styles and forms to please the purists, the basic layout is easy to comprehend, and the shops are appropriately lavish and surprisingly individualistic in appearance. The stores include a second Bijan, Camelia, Chocolat du Monde, Fendi, Nina Ricci, Saint Laurent/Rive Gauche, Emanuel Ungaro, Gianni Versace, and Louis Vuitton.

$ **CHOCOLAT DU MONDE** *Rodeo Collection, 421 North Rodeo Drive. Telephone: 276-7975.*

As more and more Americans become health- and diet-conscious, chocoholics are beginning to value quality over quantity in what they eat. But when you decide to indulge yourself, where can you find the best and the rarest of chocolates? Look no further than Chocolat du Monde, a pretty soft pink shop,

RIGHT: "The Witches' House" originally was the Irvin Willat Studio Headquarters in Culver City, but it was moved to the southeast corner of Carmelita and Walden Drives in Beverly Hills in 1931.

LEFT: Douglas Fairbanks, Sr., and Mary Pickford plant a tree at Pickfair for their publicity photographer in the 1920s. But did their fans really think that he did much work at the estate wearing those shoes—or she wearing that dress?

TOP LEFT: *Bijan, 420 Rodeo Drive. Where else would you expect to find America's haughtiest and most expensive men's store?* TOP RIGHT: *The Beverly Hills Hotel just wouldn't look like itself without the lofty palm trees and a line of shining black limousines in the driveway.* BOTTOM: *Williams-Sonoma, 438 Rodeo Drive. The cookstore raised to an art form.*

TOP: *In almost any other location this mansion at 141 South Carolwood Drive in Holmby Hills would be one of the grandest residences around. But in ultra-expensive Holmby Hills, just west of Beverly Hills, this is just another big house, though admittedly one which has been owned by pioneer movie producer Joe Schenck, Tony Curtis, and Sonny and Cher.* BOTTOM: *The East Gate to Bel Air.*

TOP: *Houses under construction in Bel Air during the 1920s.* BOTTOM: *You won't see a more impressive mansion in all of Bel Air than this French-inspired stone residence at 750 Bel Air Road. Vintage television buffs will remember that this estate was shown as the home of the Beverly Hillbillies in a popular comedy series of that name during the 1960s.*

which sells Le Notre of Paris, Catalin also of Paris, Mary of Brussels, Neuhaus also of Brussels, Lindt and Sprunglii from Switzerland, Perugina from Italy, even America's own Dilettante Chocolates from Seattle. Many of these chocolates are hand-made, and some are available in America only at this store.

To help you make your selections easier, Chocolat du Monde has tasting tables. No, that doesn't mean free samples. But for $11.50, you can get a plate of six different chocolates, a verita-ble "connoisseur's tour of chocolates," say the shop's owners. Also available are fine coffees, special chocolate pastries from Michel Richard, and chocolate mousse in an edible chocolate demitasse. Expensive, yes, but how can a chocoholic resist?

ANDERTON COURT CENTER   *328 North Rodeo Drive, Frank Lloyd Wright, architect.*

Frank Lloyd Wright on Rodeo Drive? Improbable but true. In 1953, the then eighty-five-year-old architect completed this three-story group of shops, which are arranged around a central courtyard and crowned by a futuristic—and somewhat silly-look-ing—tower. Take the pedestrian ramp to the third floor if you want a closer look at one of this master architect's more eccen-tric buildings.

CAFE SWISS   *450 North Rodeo Drive. Monday–Saturday, 11:00 A.M. to 11:00 P.M. Telephone: 274-2820. Moderate. All ma-jor credit cards. Parking in rear.*

No one has ever raved about the cooking at the Café Swiss, which serves hearty European dishes like cheese-and-onion pie, bratwurst, Wienerschnitzel, and Sauerbraten, along with tradi-tional American favorites. Instead, what brings people back to this restaurant again and again is its great value, specifically wholesome, moderately priced meals at this prime Rodeo Drive location. Skip the dark, almost-tomblike dining room in the daytime. Take a table on the patio on the rear, even if it means a short wait.

When this shoppers' paradise begins to pall, return to your car, head north on Rodeo Drive, and cross Santa Monica Boulevard. While touring the residential sections of Beverly Hills, or any residential neighborhood described in this book, do not trespass on private property and do not disturb the occupants of the houses and estates.

Just beyond the Beverly Hills Presbyterian Church, you will see a narrow alley. Turn left into the alley, and immediately behind the one-story Spanish bungalow at 507 North Rodeo Drive, you will come to a recently completed two-story Art Nouveau guesthouse, which has every sensuously flowing curve associated with this brief-lived turn-of-the-century European architectural fashion.

Only in Beverly Hills does such architectural indulgence exist, you might say to yourself. But wait. The best architectural-fantasy-become-reality is yet to come.

Continue straight down the alley until you reach the next street, which is Camden Drive. Turn right and go one block to Carmelita Avenue. Turn left, drive four blocks until you find Walden Drive. Yes, that's it: the so-called Witch's House that was built as the combination offices and dressing rooms for Irvin Willat Productions in Culver City during the mid-1920s, then moved to the southeast corner of Walden Drive and Carmelita Avenue in 1931, several years after the studio closed.

What a sight! The walls and sharply pitched roof were purposefully built to look old and sagging, as was the exterior woodwork, which was burned, charred, scraped, and left unpainted. The roof shingles were all different shapes, sizes, and colors. No two leaded-glass windows were alike, and the shutters were hung askew. Can you imagine what little children must think when they ring the front doorbell at Halloween?

Turn around and head back on Carmelita Avenue the way you came. Three blocks later, turn right on Bedford Drive and proceed three-quarters of the way down the block to 512, the former home of Clara Bow, the voluptuous, flaming red-haired "It Girl" of the 1920s. Known as "The Hottest Jazz Baby in Films," the high-spirited, sometimes earthy Clara lived up to her image offscreen. In the Chinese-style den of her bungalow, she entertained dozens of men, among them Eddie Cantor, Gary Cooper,

Bela Lugosi, and the eleven-man starting lineup of the University of Southern California football team, including tackle Marion Morrison, later named John Wayne.

Some of Clara's beaux were a little too smitten with her. She spent several evenings with Robert Savage, a football player from Yale and the son of a millionaire steel manufacturer, but she quickly tired of the young man and didn't want to see him anymore. Savage was heartbroken. In a dramatic but unsuccessful suicide attempt, he slashed his wrists and dripped his blue blood on a photograph that she had inscribed to him.

Clara was appalled. "Men don't slash their wrists," she told the press. "They use a gun!"

Turn around on Bedford Drive and drive back to Carmelita Avenue. Turn right and head down Carmelita to Canon Drive, where you turn left. With the exception of Sunset Boulevard, probably no other residential street in Beverly Hills looks more impressive than the next few blocks of Canon Drive, thanks to the perfectly maintained 80-foot-high California sand palms and 40- to 50-foot-high Mexican sand palms, which stand interspersed on both sides of the roadway.

Just after you cross the awkward six-way intersection where Canon Drive meets Beverly Drive and Elevado Avenue, you can glimpse the pink stucco Beverly Hills Hotel through the trees of a small but lovely park straight ahead. When the hotel opened in 1913, it looked out on bean fields and a handful of houses. Although the original Mission-style building still survives to the left of the main entrance, the Beverly Hills Hotel has been enlarged several times, and today it has 325 rooms, plus 20 luxurious bungalows which are scattered around the gardenlike 12-acre grounds.

The Beverly Hills Hotel probably is best known for its fabled Polo Lounge, where you really can see movie and television stars all the time. For the best celebrity-watching, avoid the pleasant outdoor tables and sit inside. Isn't that Zsa Zsa Gabor holding court at one of the semicircular dark-green booths just inside the front door? Right again.

At the intersection of Canon Drive and Sunset Boulevard, you can end your visit to Beverly Hills. Or you can turn left and head west on Sunset Boulevard in order to begin your tour of Bel Air,

145

which follows on page 162. But if you are a movie star fan or old-movies buff, you will want to see Benedict Canyon. Continue straight on Canon Drive, which becomes Benedict Canyon Drive on the other side of Sunset Boulevard.

During the 1920s and 1930s, more movie stars built palatial estates in Benedict Canyon than in any other part of Los Angeles, beginning with Douglas Fairbanks, Sr., who moved into Pickfair in 1919. Although present-day stars are scattered throughout Los Angeles now, dozens of well-known personalities still live in Benedict Canyon, which offers a convenient location, an often-rural feeling, and some of the most impressive houses in Beverly Hills.

Two blocks above Sunset Boulevard, turn left on Roxbury Drive, a gently curving street of large 1930s and 1940s homes, whose celebrity residents have included:

#1023   formerly Agnes Moorehead
#1020   formerly Ira Gershwin
#1004   Peter Falk
#1002   formerly Jack Benny
#1000   Lucille Ball
918   Jimmy Stewart

Turn around and drive back to Benedict Canyon Drive, where you turn left and proceed one block to Summit Drive, where you turn right.

On your right, notice 1018 Summit Drive: In the 1920s and 1930s, cowboy star Tom Mix lived in this then-Georgian-style mansion, which was totally modernized twenty-five years ago. Just as a cowboy brands his cattle, Mix put his initials everywhere he could find the space: on the gates to the driveway, on the front door of the house, over every fireplace. Mix even installed a neon sign with the initials TM on the roof of the house until his neighbors made him take it down.

Displaying the same flamboyant decorative spirit, Mix installed an illuminated fountain in his dining room, and at the push of a button, it sprayed water in different colors. When Mix's favorite horse, Tony, died, he turned its tail into a service bell-pull. But the mansion's *pièces de résistance* were the his and hers parlors on either side of the front entrance hall. One parlor obviously belonged to the King of the Cowboys: a 20-foot-high room with a beamed ceiling, silver-embossed saddles resting on sawhorses, a small arsenal of rifles and guns on display, and a collection of medals and trophies. The other parlor, furnished in Louis XVI-*cum*-1920s style, had been set aside for Vicki, the fourth Mrs. Mix, a former cowgirl and actress who then fancied herself a French duchess.

Unlike some actors who left their screen persona at the studio, Tom Mix was the boisterous cowboy all the time. During the christening party for his daughter at this Summit Drive mansion, Mix got roaring drunk, had a knock-down, drag-out fight in the finest Wild West tradition with cowboy actor Art Accord, and then rode his horse up the main stairs to the second floor, hollering and firing his gun into the ceiling all the way.

On your left, 1033 Summit Drive: In the mid-1930s, British actor Ronald Colman bought silent star Corinne Griffith's Tudor-style mansion, just down the hill from Pickfair. With its half-timbered walls, mullioned windows, and sloping slate roof, what home could be more appropriate for the leader of Hollywood's substantial British contingent? To heighten the illusion of Olde England, Colman ripped out the decidedly Southern California bougainvilleas and oleanders and planted yew hedges, which he formally trimmed. Then he purchased Chippendale and Sheraton furniture and hung eighteenth- and nineteenth-century British paintings in many of the rooms.

At first, Colman lived in this house by himself, probably because his first marriage had ended badly and he wasn't ready for another romance just yet. But events overtook Colman's second bachelorhood. In the late 1930s, he started seeing actress Benita Hume, who coincidentally lived in a little Spanish house behind his own. Colman installed a big oak door in the wall between the two properties so that they could discreetly visit back and forth. In 1938, Benita Hume became the second Mrs. Colman, and she moved up the hill and into the big house.

On your left, 1085 Summit Drive: In 1923, Charlie Chaplin built a Spanish-style mansion, which sits hidden from view at the end of this driveway. Although Chaplin was already a millionaire many times over, he was notoriously frugal, especially with the furnishing of this house.

147

For the first year after Chaplin moved in alone, the mansion was almost bare, except for some motley pieces here and there, carried over from the cheap rooms that he had rented in downtown Los Angeles six or eight years earlier. Rather than spend more money, Chaplin called one of the big Los Angeles department stores and asked them to send beds, dressers, and tables to fill the second-floor guest bedrooms. The store did that, but Chaplin never paid the bill. Six months later, the store repossessed the furniture. That created a problem. Chaplin needed furniture for the guest rooms again. He called another department store, and they sent the necessary beds, dressers, and tables. But Chaplin didn't pay this bill either, and six months later, the second store came to the house and took all the furniture back.

Chaplin's greatest false economy, however, was the house itself. To save money on its construction, he used his studio carpenters when they weren't busy making sets. This seemed like a sensible plan, but it turned out to be a mistake. His carpenters had become so accustomed to putting together temporary sets that they had forgotten how to build a permanent structure. No sooner had Chaplin moved into his new house than little things started to go wrong. Paneling split. Ornamental trim fell off the walls. Doors came loose from their hinges. Floors started to squeak. To Chaplin's chagrin, his friends and neighbors started calling his Summit Drive mansion "Breakaway House."

In 1982, actor George Hamilton purchased this property, hence the initial "H" on the driveway gate.

On your left, "Pickfair," 1143 Summit Drive, which is visible through the stone gates at the entrance to the driveway. In the 1920s and 1930s, Douglas Fairbanks, Sr.'s and Mary Pickford's Pickfair was the most famous home in America, even more famous than Warren G. Harding's or Calvin Coolidge's distinctly dull White House. Fairbanks and Pickford were two of Hollywood's biggest and most enduring stars as well as the nation's most popular couple, in part thanks to their small army of publicists who gave the press just enough information and photographs to make fans believe that they really knew what the two stars were like and how they lived. The newspapers and fan mag-

azines dutifully reported who came to dinner, how Mary rear-
ranged the living room furniture, what Doug gave Mary for her
birthday.

Millions of fans bought this act. They spoke of Fairbanks and
Pickford as Doug and Mary, just as if they were close friends. And
the public knew that the estate was called Pickfair, because the
press had combined parts of Fairbanks and Pickford when Mary
moved into the house, which Doug already occupied, after their
March 28, 1920, marriage.

Although Pickfair was a handsome estate, it was a surprisingly modest residence for two top stars who were earning
$1,000,000 a year *apiece* in those days before heavy income
taxes. Except for its basement screening room, where Doug and
Mary showed their films to guests after dinner, the mock-Tudor-
style house did not look that much different from the residences
of most upper-middle-class Los Angeles families: large entrance
hall, living room, dining room, breakfast room, kitchen, and servants' quarters on the first floor; five bedrooms on the second
floor; and a billiard room in the attic. Most of the rooms were
filled with expensive copies of Jacobean-style or eighteenth-
century French furniture that were sold in sets at fashionable Los
Angeles department stores.

The heavily landscaped 14-acre grounds were distinctly more
extravagant than the house, because they included a 55-by-100-
foot swimming pool with a sandy beach along one side, a series
of canoe ponds, and a six-stall stable so that Doug and Mary
could ride their horses into the then-empty hills near the estate.

But the house and its grounds were merely the backdrop,
indeed the stage set, for Doug and Mary's much-publicized pri-
vate lives. Beginning in the early 1920s, they entertained much
of the world's remaining royalty, including King Alfonso XIII of
Spain, Lord and Lady Mountbatten, the Duke and Duchess of
Sutherland, the Duke of York, the King and Queen of Siam, the
Crown Prince of Japan, and Crown Princess Fredericka of
Prussia.

Nor did the King and Queen of Hollywood, as Doug and Mary
were affectionately known, limit their celebrity guests only to
royalty. Any big name would do. At various times, Jack Demp-

sey, Albert Einstein, Amelia Earhart, F. Scott Fitzgerald, Henry Ford, Walter Johnson, Babe Ruth, and H. G. Wells ate dinner or stayed for several days at Pickfair.

Occasionally, Doug and Mary's, actually it was Doug's, fascination with nobility backfired. An American-born Italian countess, Dorothy Taylor di Frasso, came for a weekend and stayed for more than a year. And don't forget the visit of Princess Vera Romanoff. The Princess was staying at the Biltmore Hotel in downtown Los Angeles, and she called Pickfair to ask if she could meet Doug and Mary. They couldn't have been more flattered and sent one of their Rolls-Royces to bring the Princess for the weekend. The Princess enjoyed every minute of her stay, thanked Doug and Mary for their hospitality Sunday night, and returned to her secretary's job in Santa Monica the next morning.

By the early 1930s, Pickfair was losing its near-magic aura, partly because Doug's and Mary's movie careers were ending. At age fifty, Doug could no longer convincingly play the dashing swashbucklers, which made his worldwide reputation in the 1920s. Nor could forty-year-old Mary get away with appearing as a teenage girl or young woman anymore.

In addition, their much-idolized marriage was coming apart. Doug was chasing other women. Mary started drinking heavily. A year after Mary divorced Doug in 1936, she married actor Buddy Rogers, who moved into Pickfair, but the earlier excitement was gone. Mary Pickford seemed to sense this, because she sold sections of the grounds to real estate developers through the years, even though she was a millionaire many times over.

Following Mary Pickford's death in 1979, real estate and sports entrepreneur Jerry Buss bought the house and the remaining three acres for more than $5,000,000. With a $1,000,000 down payment and a twenty-year mortgage on the balance of the purchase price, Buss' monthly mortgage payments are $37,261.77.

After you pass the old Pickfair gates, keep to the left as you follow Summit Drive until you reach Pickfair Way. Drive a few hundred yards on Pickfair Way until it intersects San Ysidro Drive, where you turn left. Don't miss 1155 San Ysidro, which has been the home of actor-dancer Fred Astaire since the 1930s.

150

When San Ysidro intersects Tower Road, just before it reaches busy Benedict Canyon Drive, turn right onto Tower. Where Tower Road meets Tower Grove Road, turn left onto Tower Grove, a narrow winding street that heads up into these eucalyptus and chaparral-covered hills. Isn't it amazing that such a peaceful rural environment survives just minutes from the Beverly Hills Hotel and Rodeo Drive?

Where Tower Grove Road meets Seabright Place on the right-hand side, park your car and admire the view of "downtown Beverly Hills" and Century City below.

"Home of the Stars," 1400 Tower Grove Road, demolished, which was located on the other side of Tower Grove from the scenic overlook: Despite their relative newness, some Beverly Hills houses have complicated genealogies just like Europe's royal families, with one star following another at the same address because of frequent marriages and divorces as well as career swings up and down.

Until 1982, this eucalyptus-shaded hillside was the site of a charming 1920s Spanish-style house, which had no fewer than five successive celebrity owners: romantic silent star John Gilbert, who carried on his brief but torrid affair with Greta Garbo here in the 1920s; stage and movie actress Miriam Hopkins; *Gone With the Wind* producer David O. Selznick and actress Jennifer Jones; Warner Brothers' head Ted Ashley; and, most recently, Elton John. In 1981 Elton John sold the property to a Los Angeles businessman, who subsequently demolished the house so that he could build a larger house on this dramatic site.

Drive up Seabright Place to number 1400, the former John Barrymore estate, Belle Vista. Although Barrymore was a famed stage and movie actor, whose best-known films included *Dr. Jekyll and Mr. Hyde* (1920), *Grand Hotel* (1932), and *Twentieth Century* (1934), he could also have been an architect, considering his never-ending construction projects at Belle Vista. When Barrymore bought this eight-acre estate in 1927, the only building was a modest five-room Spanish-style house. Ten years and several million dollars later, the estate had grown to sixteen separate buildings, totaling fifty-five rooms, with several more structures underway.

Unlike most other 1920s movie stars, Barrymore's taste was

151

remarkably traditional. The Marriage House, which Barrymore built after his 1928 wedding to actress Dolores Costello, was an attractive Spanish house with oak doors, whitewashed walls hung with old prints, and tile floors covered with Oriental rugs. The upstairs drawing room was particularly handsome. Several mulberry-colored rugs lay on the pegged wood floors. Paintings and tapestries decorated the oak-paneled walls. The fireplace mantel was marble, the drapes were gold brocade, and the furniture was a mixture of antiques. The adjacent dining room was octagonal, and a pink Dresden china chandelier that had reputedly belonged to Austrian Archduke Francis Ferdinand hung from the ceiling.

For all its good design, the Marriage House occasionally reflected Barrymore's eccentricities. Barrymore had a secret hideaway where he could get away from his family, his friends, and the ringing of the telephone. Above his bedroom, he built a small tower, with a trapdoor and a ladder he could pull up after himself. Even though the ceiling was low and the room got hot on sunny days, Barrymore loved this part of the house. "This was my sanctum sanctorum," he once said, "my monastic retreat, my blessed hideaway from the world of idiocy."

But John Barrymore's greatest passion at Belle Vista was caring for his animals, which included a monkey named Clementine, opossums, South American kinkajous, mouse deer, dozens of Siamese cats, and dozens of dogs, including eleven greyhounds, several Saint Bernards, and several Kerry blue terriers. For his three hundred different birds, Barrymore built a large aviary, complete with natural and artificial trees, leaf patterns on the glass, birdbaths, fountains, and nesting places. When the structure was finished, Barrymore put a granite bench and two cast-iron cemetery chairs under a tree, where he sat for hours watching his flock. This was the one place where he didn't smoke cigarettes or his pipe. Nor did he mind the droppings that inevitably fell on his hair and clothing when the birds perched on the tree branches above.

Unfortunately, the story of John Barrymore's charming Belle Vista has an unhappy ending, as did the actor's life. By the mid-1930s, Barrymore's career was declining and his drinking was increasing. As fewer and fewer good parts came his way, Barrymore's income dropped off, and he could no longer afford to maintain Belle Vista. In 1937, Barrymore declared bankruptcy, and Belle Vista was put up for auction. No one bought the increasingly rundown property. Shortly after the Japanese bombed Pearl Harbor, Barrymore offered Belle Vista to the U.S. Army as a place to install antiaircraft guns to protect Beverly Hills from enemy attack. But the Army didn't want Belle Vista either, and Barrymore still owned the estate when he died in 1942.

Turn around and drive down Seabright Place. Turn left on Tower Grove Road, then right on Tower Road. Don't miss 1158 Tower Road, the former home of Spencer Tracy; number 1139, the former home of Artur Rubinstein; and 1136, the home of Juliet Prowse.

When Tower Road reaches Benedict Canyon Drive, turn right on Benedict Canyon. About three-quarters of a mile later, turn left on Cielo Drive. On your left, notice 10050 Cielo Drive, where the Charles Manson gang murdered Sharon Tate, Abigail Folger, Voytek Frykowski, and Jay Sebring on August 9, 1969.

Proceed farther up Cielo Drive until you reach Bella Drive. Turn right and follow this treacherously narrow road a short distance. Straight ahead you will come to the gates of Falcon Lair, the former estate of Rudolph Valentino at 1436 Bella Drive.

No 1920s star ever excited more curiosity or inflamed more passions than Rudolph Valentino, who became an overnight sensation when he played the part of young Julio in *The Four Horsemen of the Apocalypse* in 1921, then starred in *The Sheik* (1921), *Blood and Sand* (1922), and *Son of the Sheik* (1926). Even on this remote, once-empty hilltop above Beverly Hills, Valentino's fans would not leave him alone, and he built a wall around the house in order to gain some badly needed privacy. But a wall would not stop the women who were desperate for a glimpse of their idol. Just one hour of lovemaking would be enough to carry them through an entire lifetime, they told the guards who caught them climbing over the floodlit wall or prowling through the house itself.

153

Just what did these frenzied trespassers see? From the outside, the house was a typical 1920s Spanish-style hacienda, except that it was painted taupe, a then-fashionable shade of beige. But inside the house, Valentino acted out his decorative fantasies with complete abandon, spending hundreds of thousands of 1920s dollars in the process.

First, Valentino painted almost all the rooms taupe. Then he carpeted the entire house, except for the entrance hall and the dining room, in seamless Axminster wool carpeting, also in taupe. He filled the living room, dining room, library, and office on the first floor, plus the two downstairs guest rooms, with expensive antiques and would-be antiques: Turkish and Arabian furniture, several dozen fifteenth- and sixteenth-century Florentine chairs, a fifteenth-century French throne, carved Spanish screens, Oriental rugs, as well as a jumble of armor, swords, and guns.

In a complete reversal of style, Valentino decorated his downstairs bedroom suite in the latest Moderne look, and the color scheme was anything but taupe, followed by more taupe. The king-size bed had massive gold ball feet, and the headboard was lacquered dark blue. The sheets, pillowcases, and bedspread were crocus yellow—all the better to set off Valentino's several dozen pairs of yellow Japanese silk pajamas. On either side of the bed stood bright orange lacquered Moderne cabinets with the same gold ball feet. The two dressers were lacquered dark blue, and the overstuffed settee and upholstered armchair were covered in black satin. For the absolute height of 1920s bedroom decadence, the built-in perfume lamp on the orange lacquered round pedestal table at the foot of the bed filled the room with fragrance whenever the light was turned on.

After Valentino died in 1926, Falcon Lair was offered for sale at auction, but no one bid on the property. Valentino's fans, however, did not desert his memory. Except for the guards at the estate, the morbid curiosity seekers would have taken the house and grounds apart piece by piece for souvenirs. As it was, some guards made a quick buck from the faithful who stood at Falcon Lair's closed gates by selling them silverware, candles, even articles of clothing guaranteed to have come from the now-empty house. The favorite relics were feathers from Valentino's pillow.

In 1934, Falcon Lair was finally sold for $18,000, a pittance compared to what Valentino had spent to buy, landscape, and redecorate the estate. Subsequently, the property had several owners in rapid succession until tobacco heiress Doris Duke bought Falcon Lair in 1953. She seldom occupies the house, but she remains the current owner.

Retrace your route to Falcon Lair: down Bella Drive, left on Cielo, and right on Benedict Canyon. About a half mile after you turn onto Benedict Canyon, you come to Greenacres Place. Turn right on Greenacres and follow this short street to the gates of the Italian Renaissance-style mansion at the dead end.

Straight ahead, on the top of the hillock, stands Greenacres, the former Harold Lloyd mansion. When silent film comedian Lloyd moved into Greenacres in 1928, no other movie star's estate was more extravagant or more pleasingly designed. The mansion consisted of forty rooms and twenty-six bathrooms, arranged around a central courtyard. The sunken living room boasted a gold-leaf coffered ceiling, fine oak paneling, and a Renaissance-style fireplace, plus a hidden movie screen and a pipe organ so that Lloyd could show his films at home. Nearby were the formal dining room, a small French-style drawing room, a music room, a library, and a garden room whose walls and arched ceiling were covered with painted vines, birds, and flowers. A wood-paneled elevator ascended to the ten bedrooms on the second floor.

The 20-acre grounds contained twelve gardens, and each one followed a different theme. The athletic Floyd even built handball and tennis courts, an 800-foot-long canoe pond, and a nine-hole golf course. Jack Warner, one of the Warner Brothers, also had a nine-hole golf course at his estate next door, and sometimes he and Lloyd erected a temporary walkway over the fence so that their guests could play all eighteen holes.

But what has happened to all these beautiful grounds, you may wonder. With 20 acres, Greenacres must have included more land than what we see around the mansion today. You're right. Several years after Lloyd's death in 1971, Middle Eastern investors purchased the property, and they subdivided eleven of the remaining sixteen acres into building lots, leaving the mansion and the surrounding five acres intact.

155

Greenacres Place is the estate's former driveway, and the large houses on either side stand on the site of the former gardens. When you drive back down the hill, the houses along Benedict Canyon on your left have replaced the golf course and canoe pond.

Turn right on Benedict Canyon Drive. When you reach Sunset Boulevard, the Beverly Hills tour is over. If you wish, you may turn right on Sunset Boulevard and begin the Bel Air tour.

11
Holmby Hills/Bel Air Tour

START: *Sunset Boulevard and Benedict Canyon Drive, just west of the Beverly Hills Hotel.*

TIME: *Approximately two hours.*

Holmby Hills Background: As you drive west on Sunset Boulevard you will leave Beverly Hills at the end of the first S curve and enter Los Angeles. But this is not just any part of Los Angeles. Between the Beverly Hills/Los Angeles boundary and Beverly Glen Boulevard, a distance of one mile, Sunset Boulevard passes through Holmby Hills, which is uniformly the most expensive neighborhood in all Los Angeles, certainly more costly than Beverly Hills as a whole. While touring the residential sections of Holmby Hills and Bel Air, or any residential neighborhood described in this book, do not trespass on private property and do not disturb the occupants of the houses and estates.

What makes Holmby Hills so desirable? This district consists only of mansions and estates, without any shops, apartment buildings, or small houses. Thanks to its hilly topography and carefully tended landscaping, Holmby Hills has a countrified and

157

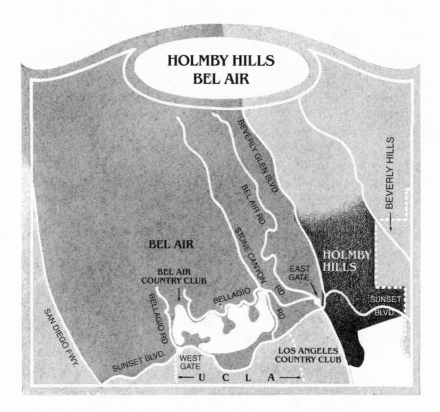

private mood, even though it is only a five-minute drive to Rodeo Drive or Century City. Furthermore, most tourists and Angelenos don't know about Holmby Hills, because it is situated between the far more famous Beverly Hills and Bel Air. And if outsiders have heard about the area, they face a difficult time finding their way around the winding narrow roads.

Heading west on Sunset Boulevard, notice the driveway at number 10,000, which was one of the houses in which Judy Garland attempted suicide.

Just beyond 10,000, turn left on South Carolwood Drive. Be careful. Most traffic is moving overly fast for this curving stretch of Sunset Boulevard, and you will not find a separate lane for the left turn across the opposing two lanes of traffic onto South Carolwood. To turn left here, give the other drivers plenty of warning by slowing down and switching on your left-turn signal as soon as you see the driveway for 10,000 Sunset.

After arriving on South Carolwood, you will see the gate and pink masonry wall for an estate on the corner, which has a 10,100 Sunset Boulevard address. This eight-bedroom Spanish-style mansion, which was built by Rudy Vallee, was Jayne Mansfield's "Pink Palace" in the 1950s and 1960s.

When Jayne said pink, she meant it. The wall around the estate, the stucco façade, the rooms, and wall-to-wall carpeting on the floors and the ceilings of the entrance hall and living room, the heart-shaped swimming pool, the heart-shaped bathtub, even the heart-shaped toilet seats were all pink. Only occasionally did another color creep into the house, such as in the living room with its plush purple-upholstered sofa, white-and-gold piano, crystal chandeliers, religious statuary, and pictures of Jayne.

Although Jayne Mansfield may have looked and acted the part of the dumb blonde, she knew how to get the most for her money in remodeling the Pink Palace. Her Hungarian muscle-man husband, Mickey Hargitay, had been a builder, and he completed or supervised most of the work. Then Jayne's press agent, Jim Bryon, asked 1,500 furniture and building supply houses for free samples. Think of the honor, he told them, of having your—fill in the blank—as a part of the Pink Palace. The pitch worked. Jayne Mansfield received more than $150,000 worth of free merchandise.

Singer Engelbert Humperdinck presently lives in the Pink Palace.

At the end of this short dead-end street, peer through the elaborate iron gates of 141 South Carolwood. What an important-looking part-Spanish/part-Italian Renaissance-style mansion. The grounds are particularly lovely: the wide expanse of carefully trimmed lawn, the ornamental flowerbeds, the orange trees, and a splashing fountain.

Producer/studio executive Joseph Schenck built this house in 1934 shortly after his divorce from silent star Norma Talmadge. Apparently Schenck always liked actresses. When Marilyn Monroe was a starlet in the early 1950s, she lived in the estate's guesthouse, reportedly so that she could be the on-premises girl friend for the aging Schenck. After Schenck's death, the estate's owners have been Tony Curtis, followed by Sonny and Cher, followed by a foreign businessman.

After seeing 141 South Carolwood, return to Sunset Boulevard and turn left. The next street is Charing Cross Road. Turn left.

Do not miss 10236 Charing Cross, the home of Hugh Hefner. When guests arrive at the Playboy Mansion, they must speak into a microphone at the beginning of the driveway. Only then does one of Hefner's minions open the gates by remote control. Little do visitors realize that they also have been checked out by a television camera concealed in the nearby shrubs. Just after you pass the Playboy Mansion driveway, you can catch a glimpse of the gray Tudor-style mansion on the hillside above.

Beyond the Playboy Mansion, notice the massive steel framework that supports a tennis court at another estate. Rich Angelenos will do anything to have a north-south tennis court.

When you reach Mapleton Drive in a short distance, turn left. Notice 282 South Mapleton, a handsome Spanish-style mansion with definite 1930s Moderne touches, such as the crisply detailed rectangular front entrance and semicircular arch over the driveway. Several blocks farther ahead, 594 South Mapleton is the former home of Bing Crosby.

At this point, turn around and drive north on Mapleton, past Charing Cross, all the way to Sunset Boulevard. Go slowly. At 232 South Mapleton, on your right, you can glimpse the former home of Humphrey Bogart and Lauren Bacall. Just ahead and also on the right, study 130 South Mapleton. This modern house is supposed to look expensive and impressive. But what architectural style is it? Do you have any idea?

At Sunset Boulevard, turn left. If you feel like exploring a little known but fascinating part of Los Angeles, turn right on Beverly Glen Boulevard, just past the bend in Sunset Boulevard. Otherwise, continue west on Sunset Boulevard for a few hundred yards until you come to Bel Air Road, where you turn right and enter Bel Air.

BEVERLY GLEN SIDE TRIP: Few spots in Los Angeles offer a more charming or varied setting than Beverly Glen, a steep-sided and narrow canyon which separates Beverly Hills and Holmby Hills from Bel Air. At first, Beverly Glen Boulevard passes Beverly Hills-style mansions, complete with the requisite lawns, hedges, and tennis courts. But about a half mile above Sunset Boulevard, the neighborhood takes on a far different look, much like Laurel Canyon. The houses are far more modest, and they range from charming early-twentieth-century cottages to strikingly contemporary redwood-sided residences. In many spots, Beverly Glen is so narrow that these houses stand on postage-stamp-size lots which are wedged between the road and the walls of the canyon.

North of the Glen Market at Crater Street, a few narrow roads lead off Beverly Glen Boulevard into the nearby hills. Take one. You will see Beverly Glen at its most delightful: more Hobbit-scale houses, lots of shrubs and flowers, and an uncommon sense of tranquillity.

About 2.5 miles north of Sunset Boulevard, Beverly Glen widens and the road becomes four lanes wide. The intimacy of lower Beverly Glen is gone. You might as well be driving through any of Los Angeles' newer affluent suburbs. Unless you want to head up to Mulholland Drive for the view, turn around on one of the side streets and return to Sunset Boulevard. On your way down the hill, you might want to eat dinner or Sunday brunch at the **Café Four Oaks,** a casual Continental-style restaurant in a turn-of-the-century house at 2181 North Beverly Glen Boulevard. Telephone: 474-9317. Or you may want to stop in the **Glen Market** at 1601 North Beverly Glen for a snack or something cold to drink. You won't pass anything so plebeian as a market in Bel Air, which is your next destination.

ADVICE: If Beverly Glen has a flaw, it is too much traffic. Beverly Glen Boulevard is one of the few direct routes from West Los Angeles over the Santa Monica Mountains into the San Fernando Valley. You should not, therefore, drive slowly on this road at any time of day. For sightseeing purposes, avoid heading north on Beverly Glen in the evening rush hour. The road is filled with drivers anxious to go home to the Valley.

When you reach Sunset Boulevard, turn right. In a few hundred feet, turn right on Bel Air Road and drive through the gates. Pretty impressive looking, aren't they?

BEL AIR BACKGROUND: Oil millionaire Alfonzo Bell offered the first lots in Bel Air for sale in 1922. He selected the name Bel Air because it roughly translated from French as "beautiful place" yet incorporated his family name as well. According to Bell's advertisements, Bel Air would be "the crowning achievement of suburban development," and he meant this. With architect Mark Daniel's help, Bell carved roads out of the hillsides and dug underground water, sewage, and electric lines. Then he planted thousands of shrubs and trees.

Next Bell divided the first 200-acre tract, just west of Beverly Glen and north of Sunset Boulevard, into several-acre parcels, nothing smaller, and he encouraged buyers to purchase larger lots. He laid out polo fields, tennis courts, and an 18-hole golf course, which became the Bel Air Country Club. In order to attract the horsey set, Bell built the Bel Air Stables on Stone Canyon Road and prepared 65 miles of bridle paths through the hills.

As one last splendid gesture, Bell erected a large, handsome gate at the Bel Air Road entrance to the community, just as rich men installed gates at the head of driveways to their estates. Uniformed guards checked cars in and out of the neighborhood here, and a private police force patrolled the streets and escorted visitors from the gates up the sometimes-confusing roads to their destination.

In the beginning, Bell refused to sell land to "movie people," along with Jews, blacks, and Orientals. This no-movie-people policy worked just fine in the prosperous 1920s, but it proved disastrous during the Depression. So few businessmen wanted to buy land and build mansions that Bel Air almost went bankrupt. The private guards at the gate disappeared in an economy move. Bell couldn't afford to be so selective anymore, and his real estate agents discreetly welcomed inquiries from film stars and studio executives. They were some of the only people in Los Angeles who could afford—and would pay—Bel Air prices.

Mary Duncan, a Broadway-actress-turned-film-performer, reportedly was the first movie person to get in. Then Colleen

Moore, who had portrayed flappers in the 1920s, bought an estate on St. Pierre Road. in 1935, Warner Baxter, who played the popular Cisco Kid roles and got the starring part of Julian Marsh in *42nd Street* (1933), built a Tudor-style stone mansion at 688 Nimes Road. These stars were the advance guard. By the 1940s, movie people were swarming into Bel Air.

Today, all kinds of people live in the community, not just the American WASPS that Bell wanted, but also Jews and a few blacks, plus Europeans, Middle Easterners, and Asians. The only common denominator in Bel Air seems to be money, lots of it.

Don't tell anyone, but not all Bel Air is created equal. The streets around the East Gate, which you have just entered have always been more desirable than those around the West Gate, which is located 1.5 miles farther west on Sunset Boulevard. Another important distinction is how far up into the hills, that is away from Sunset Boulevard, the house is located. After the Second World War, some of the winding streets in the upper reaches of Bel Air filled up with ranch-style houses, albeit on a more lavish scale than in the typical middle-class suburb.

The difference between the estate area near Sunset Boulevard and the postwar houses in the hills is so extreme that realtors—as well as the residents of the far more expensive prewar estates—often speak of Old Bel Air and New Bel Air. Regardless of where they live, however, every resident of the neighborhood enjoys the privilege of driving through one of the two gates along Sunset Boulevard on their way home.

After entering Bel Air's East Gate, continue straight ahead up Bel Air Road. Some of the several-million-dollar-and-up mansions are visible from the street. But most are well hidden behind thick hedges or the rolling topography. All you can see is a driveway leading to a set of closed gates, plus the ubiquitous signs saying that the Bel Air Patrol or another private guard service protects the property. More than a few estates have their own armed guards and attack dogs.

Occasionally, the iron gates on the driveways swing open, and a gleaming Rolls-Royce emerges from its pampered lair. Otherwise, nearly all the cars and trucks on Bel Air Road and nearby streets belong to tourists or to service personnel, like

163

gardeners, caterers, interior decorators, and poolmen. You might even see the mobile dog trimmer's van or the Mercedes mechanic who makes house calls.

Be sure to stop to admire the French-style stone mansion at 750 Bel Air Road, which stands in full view of the street. First you see the gates to the property, then a long rectangular formal garden with the driveway on either side, and finally the elegant two-story limestone house itself. Don't be surprised if another car pulls up while you are looking at this mansion. This is the best-known house in Bel Air. On weekend afternoons, dozens of cars stop in front of the gates, and tourists as well as Angelenos jump out and take photographs. No, these people are not connoisseurs of fine French architecture. Instead, most remember that the estate was used as the home of television's "Beverly Hillbillies" in the 1960s.

The story of 750 Bel Air Road proves the old adage that "truth is stranger than fiction." The builder was Lynn Atkinson, who had become rich completing dams, bridges, and tunnels throughout the West. In 1935, Atkinson decided that his comfortable home at 324 South Muirfield Road in Hancock Park wasn't good enough for him anymore. So he bought this 12-acre piece of land and hired architect Sumner Spaulding to prepare plans for a 40-room mansion. Atkinson didn't tell his wife, Berenice, what he was doing. He wanted the house to be a surprise.

Three years and $2,000,000 later, Atkinson had completed his French-style mansion, which looked as though it had been carried from a fashionable Parisian boulevard to a Bel Air hillside. As befitted a contractor's home, the walls were reinforced concrete, faced with Indiana limestone, and the roof was copper. The cast-iron drainpipes were concealed in the walls so that they did not mar the beauty of the façade.

The front door opened into a 20-by-30-foot reception hall with a solid beige marble floor, frescoed walls, and a ceiling that rose three full stories to a skylight and a Baccarat crystal chandelier with 120 lights. Nearby, the 30-by-70-foot living room had walnut parquet floors, damask-covered walls, a marble fireplace, and an organ console. The ceilings were 18 feet high, and a row of French doors opened onto a terrace along the back of the house overlooking the city below.

Atkinson's home was built into a steep hillside and, therefore, it was two stories tall in front and four in back. The floor below the main one contained a 20-by-40-foot ballroom with a maple floor, marble and mirrored walls, and a gold-leaf ceiling; a card room; a billiard room; plus one furniture vault, one linen vault, one crystal vault, one china vault, and two silver vaults.

The mansion was lavish down to the smallest detail. Every room had gold doorknobs, including the first-floor dining room, library, breakfast room, men's and women's cloakrooms, and garden room, which had a fountain in the middle of its dark-green marble floor. Atkinson's mansion quickly became known around Los Angeles as "the house of the golden doorknobs." But gold was visible everywhere—in the built-in mirror frames, ceilings, organ grilles, even bathroom fixtures. And because he had invested in oil wells, Atkinson even installed a gold derrick in his bathroom to pump water into his bathtub.

After Atkinson had surreptitiously finished his house, he thought about exactly the right way to show the estate to his wife. He couldn't just drive her over in their car. So he decided to throw a housewarming party and not tell Berenice anything until she saw the house that evening, brilliantly lit, filled with dance music, and thronged with guests. As the Atkinsons drove over the Bel Air for the party, Berenice asked her husband who the hosts were. "It's a surprise," he replied, "but you know them."

When the Atkinsons arrived at the house, the courtyard was filled with dozens of Packards and Cadillacs dropping off fashionably dressed men and women at the front door. Atkinson and his wife got out of their car and walked into the three-story-high reception hall where a band was playing. Still blissfully unaware of her surprise, Berenice Atkinson turned to her proud husband and whispered: 'Who would ever live in a house like this? It's so pretentious."

Atkinson was crestfallen but managed to say: "Well, then, let's go. We don't have to stay at this party." And they left their own housewarming celebration.

When Berenice Atkinson later learned the truth, she made a more thorough inspection of the estate. But that didn't change her original opinion, and the Atkinsons continued to live on Muirfield Road, while he unhappily paid real estate taxes and guards' salaries for the unoccupied "house of the golden door-knobs." In July 1945 Atkinson sold the estate to hotel millionaire Arnold Kirkeby for $200,000.

After admiring the Atkinson/Kirkeby residence, continue driving up Bel Air Road, noticing number 783, which was the home of singer-actress Jeanette MacDonald. Just beyond 948 Bel Air Road, you will see a view of Los Angeles to your right. Don't stop here. The road is so narrow that you will hold up traffic, and besides, you can enjoy the same sight farther ahead. Don't miss 1001 Bel Air Road on your left, the former residence of Howard Hughes, presently the home of Zsa Zsa Gabor.

Immediately after passing 1200 Bel Air Road you come to Bel Air Place on your left where you can park your car briefly, then walk across Bel Air Road and study the spectacular view: Look down into virtually undeveloped Beverly Glen. The hills on the opposite side are part of Beverly Hills. Straight ahead and to your right, you will see downtown Los Angeles' office towers, smog willing.

Return to your car and keep driving up Bel Air Road, which now runs along the top of a narrow mountain ridge. The neighborhood has obviously changed. Gone are the estates and the foliage-lined curving roads. You have reached the New Bel Air: smaller and newer ranch-style houses and fairly small lots with a minimum of landscaping.

Drive along Bel Air Road as far as you wish, being sure to look at the hills on either side, then turn around and follow Bel Air Road back down the hill until you come to a Y-shaped intersection with Nimes Road, just a little beyond 948 Bel Air Road.

Nimes Road is part of the prime Old Bel Air estate district. Drive slowly and enjoy all the mansions, when you can see them, and the trees and flowering hedges along the road. Don't miss 688 Nimes Road, which was built by 1930s screen idol Warner Baxter and later became the home of Jack Ryan, the inventor of Mattell's Barbie and Chatty Cathy dolls. When Ryan purchased this five-acre estate in the mid-1970s, he built a drawbridge to the front door of the 1930s Tudor-style mansion, hired UCLA students as servants and dressed them in English livery, and installed more than 150 telephones around the house and grounds. During his first year at this estate, Ryan also threw 150 parties, until the neighbors finally put a stop to the constant entertaining.

Where Nimes Road reaches a T-shaped intersection with St. Cloud Road, turn left on St. Cloud, which passes more mansions and estates, including number 364, formerly the residence of singer Sonny Bono, now the home of *Hustler* publisher Larry Flynt, and number 332, formerly the residence of MGM studio head Louis B. Mayer, now the home of comedian Jerry Lewis.

Follow St. Cloud Road until you come to Bel Air Road again. Turn left on Bel Air Road. At the next intersection, just before the East Gate, turn right on Bellagio Road, a mansion-lined street which runs roughly east to west, parallel and above Sunset Boulevard. When you arrive at Copa De Oro, turn right and pick up Bellagio a few hundred feet ahead on your right.

At Stone Canyon Road, turn right and drive north until you come to the Bel Air Hotel on your left at number 701. "Luxurious," "quiet," "romantic." All these adjectives are used again and again to describe big-city hotels, and in most instances, they are not much more than public relations puffery. Yet, at the Bel Air Hotel, all these words are true, and more.

Probably no other public place in Los Angeles better symbolizes the Southern California "good life." See for yourself. Drop off your car with valet parking and step across the bridge into the lush flowering gardens. On your right, you see the swan pond. Straight ahead stands the hotel: a rambling vaguely Spanish-style collection of buildings that were erected for the Bel Air Stables in the 1920s, then converted into a hotel during the 1940s. No wonder travelers who know genuine quality and individuality, as well as celebrities who really want some privacy, have been coming to the Bel Air Hotel for years. Even if you are not a guest, what better place could you find to take a short walk or to eat Sunday brunch? Reservations are necessary. Inquire about dress code.

A note about the swans: Ten years ago, the two swans disappeared from their pond. They hadn't wandered off; they had been kidnapped by a neighborhood woman. When the kidnapper called the hotel, she demanded a Doberman pinscher she had seen on the grounds earlier that day in exchange for the safe return of the swans. The woman sounded quite disappointed— and confused about what to do next—when the manager informed her that the dogs belonged to a guest, not to the hotel.

This story, however, has a happy ending. Several hours later, a distinguished-looking man drove up to the hotel in his Rolls-Royce, opened the trunk, and removed a sack containing two swans who were thoroughly frightened and looked somewhat worse for wear. His wife, he explained, sometimes did strange things when she had been drinking.

After leaving the Bel Air Hotel, turn left and drive up Stone Canyon Road to number 1231, a Tudor-style house that Judy Garland built for herself and her mother, Ethel, in 1940. This house had everything that a teenage girl could possibly want: a tennis court, a badminton court, pinball machines, even a suite for Judy on the top floor with its own separate entrance. Her bedroom also had a secret hideaway concealed behind a built-in bookcase that moved aside with the push of a button. For all its special features, though, Judy Garland never liked this house. Even though she had paid for its construction, she referred to the house as her mother's, because, she claimed, she really built it for her mother.

Turn around and head back down Stone Canyon Road, past the Bel Air Hotel, until you reach Bellagio Road, where you turn right. Shortly afterwards, notice 10615 Bellagio Road on your right, formerly the home of Cary Grant. Just beyond this vaguely Tudor-style house, you will see the entrance to UCLA's Japanese Garden on the right. This is a must for garden enthusiasts or someone who would enjoy a quiet and contemplative walk. Call UCLA's Visitors' Center at 825-4574 for hours and to make a reservation.

Continue westward on Bellagio Road until it reaches Bel Air's West Gate on Sunset Boulevard. This is the conclusion of the Holmby Hills/Bel Air tour. Turn left on Sunset Boulevard to reach Beverly Hills and Hollywood.

Postscript

Year after year, Hollywood is one of the most popular tourist attractions in Southern California. Yet when many visitors arrive expectantly on Hollywood Boulevard, they are disappointed. All they see are the footprints of the stars at the Chinese Theater, several movie memorabilia shops, and perhaps the faded Musso & Frank Grill.

You don't see many movie stars in Hollywood any longer, unless they are driving to their hillside homes. Instead you find remarkable remnants of Hollywood's "golden era" in the 1920s and 1930s, unexpected traces of Los Angeles' history, some of the city's finest—or often most offbeat—architecture, all kinds of fascinating shops for clothes, home furnishings, food, or antiques, some of Southern California's best and most innovative restaurants, and a surprising amount of virtually unspoiled open space in the hills, not to mention stirring views of Los Angeles and the San Fernando Valley from these same hills.

But Hollywood does not reveal its special places readily, in part because of its large geographic scale and often-hilly topography. Besides, Angelenos and visitors often drive past interesting places which they might see if they were on foot.

To explore Hollywood, you need time, energy, and curiosity, plus a knowledgeable friend or a guidebook that shows you the best and shuns the merely ordinary. Seeing Hollywood this way takes more planning than just driving around, but the rewards are worth the additional trouble, because Hollywood is the single most fascinating and vibrant place in all of Los Angeles.

169

Index

Index

171

Index

172

Index

Index